A God-Made Millionaire

Personal and Business Finance God's Way

Steve Main

www.SteveMain.com

Published by

VisionQuest Ministries

www.VQResources.com

$12.95

ISBN 978-0-9716489-6-8

Dedication

I thank God for all the blessing He has showered on my family and for paying me so well to manage some of His wealth. I want to thank my beautiful wife, Laura, for her tremendous loving support. I honor my parents, Frank and LaVon Main, who have always taught me that my relationship with Christ is first priority. I also thank Victor Brodt, Pastor John Jackson, Pastor Randy Brodhagen, Pastor Steve Wilson, and Pastor Dick Johnson (who was my Sunday school teacher). These men have all been mentors and provided guidance to me.

All the proceeds from the sale of this printed book will go towards God's ministries.

Table of Contents

Foreword

God wants you to be free. He sees you as you are and as you can be. He knows the end from the beginning and you want to trust Him for that. But what stops you from going where He calls you to go? **Fear.** Steve Main has learned what freedom is all about. He has learned how to face his fears and go where God is calling. I've watched Steve now for the past few years. I've seen him make God-sized decisions without fear. I've seen him trust God when there were apparent reasons not to trust. Steve has demonstrated that he understands and lives the principles of this book. He is a God-made millionaire.

In my work as a pastor, speaker, and author, I often see people gripped by the fear of the unknown. Once you read this book, you will have the essential tools to fulfill your God-given assignment in this life. You will not fear money, work, or the future. You will face what lies ahead with confidence and security. I believe this book will bring life to your soul as you receive the truth of God's Word and apply it to your circumstances. Soar to new heights based on God's Kingdom principles. Then you too can be a God-made man or woman, full of freedom and hope!

In His Grip,

Dr. John Jackson
Author of Pastorpreneur, and
Leveraging Your Leadership Style
www.pastorpreneur.com

Introduction

What is a millionaire? My financial statement showed multi-millions in net worth by the age of 38 but here I will actually suggest that there really is no such thing as a millionaire! Every human being comes into this world with absolutely nothing and that is exactly how they leave. Even the Bible teaches this reality: *"For we brought nothing into the world, and we can take nothing out of it"* (1 Timothy 6:7). No one would argue the fact that we all end up with nothing from this earth as far as material possessions go. We don't even get to keep the body we used on earth!

You might have picked up this book because you wanted to learn how to accumulate great wealth. If so, this book will teach you many pre-requisites and principles for growing and managing great wealth beyond your imagination. What is also important to learn, however, is that *motive* is the key – and a solid foundation must be built first.

Without the right motive there really is no *wealth*. Building wealth is about attitude, faith and a lack of fear. I will unpack this over the next several chapters. You might not realize that without a Biblical foundation, wealth-building is actually hindered! It is my hope that as you begin to understand the Biblical foundations on finance you will begin to see the simplicity of growing great wealth.

I saw a fascinating interview about wealth one day on Fox News. Neil Cavuto interviewed Robert Kiyosaki. Mr. Kiyosaki is the author of the book *Rich Dad Poor Dad*, a book I recommend (Time Warner Paperbacks). Kiyosaki is a great author and I highly recommend his books to you.

Evidently Mr. Kiyosaki made some comments in an article that some people felt insinuated that poor people are lazy. Mr. Kiyosaki was attempting to clarify his comments on Neil

Cavuto's show. I understood Mr. Kiyosaki to be saying that poor people do not make the choices they know they should and need to make in order to increase wealth. I will not judge whether this is or is not always the case, but I will say I believe it is *often* the case. Of course many of the e-mails sent to Neil Cavuto blasted the concept that poor people are lazy. Excuses are made such as, "I want to spend more time with my family" and "I work really hard." That might be true, but I think I spend more time with my family than most fathers and I make more money than nine out of ten dads in this country.

Looking down on wealthy individuals is a popular pastime in our country. Many people look down their noses at people with money and make accusations about their character. Many of the people who do this are insecure, lack faith and are afraid. Fear racks them and causes them to rationalize why money is bad.

People who have money and write books about money will always be criticized. This is because many people are afraid of failure and intimidated by money. Some of my readers will even dislike this book because they want to avoid the issues of money.

As you turn the page and begin the journey through this book, do so with an open mind and a willingness to change some of your attitudes and behaviors relating to money. It is my hope that you will understand more clearly what money truly is and how to grow wealth.

PART I
Understanding Money

Chapter 1:
Does God Want People To Be Poor?

There are some who say that God actually wants people to be poor! To answer the question of whether God wants people to be poor, look no further than a handful of Bible verses and a dose of common sense:

> *"All they asked was that we should continue to remember the poor, the very thing I was eager to do"* (Galatians 2:10).

> *"Cornelius, God has heard your prayer and remembered your gifts to the poor"* (Acts 10:31).

If God wanted people to be poor these verses would read something
like this:

> *"All they asked was that we should leave the poor to fend for themselves."*

> *"Cornelius, God has heard your prayer and remembered your gifts to the poor so He is going to ignore your request."*

If God wanted people to be poor He would not have instructed us to help them!

From my reading of the Bible it is apparent that God's first priority is our spiritual health and our relationship with Him:

> *"You shall not make for yourself an idol in the form of anything in heaven above or on the earth beneath or in the waters below. You shall not bow down to them or worship them; for I, the Lord your God, am a jealous God, punishing the children for the sin of the fathers to the third and fourth generation of those who hate me, but showing love to a*

thousand generations of those who love me and keep my commandments" (Exodus 20:4-6).

So the question then becomes, how healthy am I spiritually, and is there anything that is hindering my relationship with God from growing? The reality is that money can be an idol in anyone's life – and not only that, but the love and desire for money can actually do us great harm. Read what Paul says about the destructiveness of falling head over heels for money:

"People who want to get rich fall into temptation and a trap and into many foolish and harmful desires that plunge men into ruin and destruction. For the love of money is a root of all kinds of evil. Some people, eager for money, have wandered from the faith and pierced themselves with many griefs" (1 Timothy 6:9-10).

There is such power in this truth. I believe it is true and have seen it play out in people's lives. For me it is pretty simple: I do not want to get rich.

This might surprise some of my readers, especially if you picked up this book because you wanted to get rich. So let me clarify my statement.

Don't: I don't want to get rich

Do: I do want to manage hundreds of millions (even billions) of dollars for God.

It is my belief that the Bible is God's Word, and that it is truth and not opinion. Read back over the above verses. It does not say, "Some people who want to get rich..." or even, "Most people who want to get rich..." It reads, "People who want to get rich." It also does not say, "Money is a root of all kinds of evil." The verse is often quoted this way! I've heard people in all walks of life misquote the verse in this way because it sounds striking and because it can often make the point the speaker is trying to make more effectively. In fact, it is convenient to misquote this verse because it is easier to say, "Wealth is bad" and look down on wealthy individuals than it is to develop the disciplines and habits that wealth management requires!

Instead, the verse reads, "The *love* of money is a root of all kinds of evil" (italics mine).

God does not want us to be poor, but He has a greater concern for helping us avoid the love and unhealthy desire for money. God is not going to give us something that will destroy us!

Being a parent helps me understand this concept so much better. When my son was two years old he was very rambunctious. He was always drawn to exciting, dangerous tools and activities. But as his dad I had a huge responsibility to care for him and his rambunctiousness. I didn't let him play with knives or buzz saws no matter how much he wanted to play with them!

In a similar way, I also never want to damage my children with material objects. I always want to give them their hearts' desires but I strived to make sure that meeting those desires is not hurtful and that they are mature enough to receive them. As parents know, it is often hard *not to give* children what they want. My kids love ice cream but hate dinner. But it just makes sense: my wife Laura and I do not give our kids ice cream before dinner!

God wants to give us the desires of our heart:

"You have granted him the desire of his heart and have not withheld the requests of his lips" (Psalm 21:2).

This poetry was written by King David who had a heart similar to God's. Contrast this with David's predecessor to the throne, King Saul, who lost his riches and his rule because he would not follow God's instructions:

"But now your kingdom will not endure; the Lord has sought out a man after His own heart and appointed him leader

of His people, because you have not kept the Lord's command" (1 Samuel 13:14).

"After removing Saul, he made David their king. He testified concerning him: 'I have found David son of Jesse a man after my own heart; he will do everything I want him to do'" (Acts 13:22).

David did everything God wanted him to do, but he also did a lot of things God did not want him to do. Read the Bible, and that becomes obvious.

If we do everything God wants us to do with money I do not believe we will be poor. If our hearts' desires are the same as God's desires, He will give us those desires.

"Dear friends, if our hearts do not condemn us, we have confidence before God and receive from Him anything we ask because we obey His commands and do what pleases Him" (1 John 3:21-22).

I believe this principle and have found it true in my life and in the lives of others I know: if we do what pleases God with money He will only give us more. In fact, in time He will pour out so many blessings we will not have enough room to store them! My family and I are blessed in every area I can think of. It seems like we have to empty out our garage and closets every month. Sometimes I ask myself, "Where is all this stuff coming from?"

"For I know the plans I have for you," declares the LORD, "plans to prosper you and not to harm you, plans to give you hope and a future" (Jeremiah 29:11).

Although this specific promise in context is for the nation of Israel, I wholeheartedly believe there are specific applications for the lives of Christ-followers as well. In the previous verse God tells us what His plans are for us. It is interesting to note that God does not just have *one plan* for us but *multiple plans*. He has plans to prosper us. People who teach against wealth and criticize the wealthy often have trouble explaining why so many God-followers in the Old Testament were so wealthy and why God specifically blessed them in tangible, financial ways.

God does not have a plan to make us poor. In contrast, the more money God gives us to manage the more we can help the poor. Helping the poor often *starts* with material help – with food, clothing, health care, micro-loans and meeting other basic needs. It does not end there, but it often starts there. God wants us to help the poor and that is much easier with a significant amount of money.

You might be discouraged reading this because of some temporary or long-term setbacks that you have recently experienced. I believe that if we trust God even setbacks are part of His plan to prosper us. My setbacks have catapulted me into prosperity. Looking back on it, the setbacks I experienced were necessary. As hard as it might seem at first, try to get excited about setbacks. Remember, failure is not fatal. Anyone who is afraid of failure will stay stuck in the mud!

Whatever you do, do not fall into the temptation that wallowing in the mud is a form of "contentment." Wallowing is a form of failure, not contentment! In the next chapter I will outline what contentment is and what it is not, and how we can successfully attain contentment so that our heart does not fall head over heels in love with money.

Chapter 2: Discovering Contentment

Contentment is the key to wealth:

"Godliness with contentment is great gain" (1 Timothy 6:6).

"Keep your lives free from the love of money and be content with what you have, because God has said, "Never will I leave you; never will I forsake you" (Hebrews 13:5).

If you read the above verse in Hebrews carefully, it does not read, "Keep your lives free from money." Rather, it reads this way: "Keep your lives free from the *love* of money" (italics mine). As you have no doubt already figured out from the previous chapter, this is an important distinction! Read also what Paul writes in 1 Timothy:

"But if we have food and clothing, we will be content with that" (1 Timothy 6:8).

This verse does not say God *only* wants to give us food and clothing. Godliness with contentment is great gain. The fact is this: if we are content with little, we will avoid the pitfalls of the love of money. When God pays us well and gives us wealth we will feel incredibly rich and blessed. The author of Ecclesiastes knew this all too well:

"There was a man all alone; he had neither son nor brother. There was no end to his toil, yet his eyes were not content with his wealth. 'For whom am I toiling,' he asked, 'and why am I depriving myself of enjoyment?' This too is meaningless— a miserable business!" (Ecclesiastes 4:8)

The man described in this story was not content with his wealth. No matter how much money or possessions you might own you will never be truly "rich" without contentment. Like the man described above, we will only want more – and be miserable.

When I was a personal trainer in Palm Springs I met so many people who were gripped with fear. They worried constantly about losing their wealth. If these people would have been content with less, the fear would have been gone. Instead of worrying about what they might lose they could have been overjoyed with what they had. It was devastating to watch.

Which would you rather have, bondage to fear or freedom and joy? You may not have realized that true contentment is actually the key to freedom and joy. People who are content are not in need. People who *want* are actually the ones in need – no matter how much they have!

Anyone who is content with food and clothes will have no fear of loss. The bottom line is this: **fearless people are free to chase the dreams God gives them**. When you possess this freedom it is so much more meaningful than how many square-feet your house has or what type of restaurants you frequent. This kind of freedom serves as the antidote to the fear that I have observed in people, both in Palm Springs and everywhere else I have lived.

What I have experienced is this: fear causes many people to hang on to what they have and try to protect it. It is actually more likely that people with *little* are worshiping money more than people with *more* of it. That is a key reason people with little have little: God doesn't like money-worshipers!

If you want the contentment that is so elusive for so many people, start with confession: tell someone else that you are afraid. It might be hard at first since revealing that you are afraid is so taboo in our culture. You might be afraid of appearing *weak* but you will likely discover *strength* when you confess your fear to another person.

After you have done that, give everything away. Write a letter or a contract if that helps you. Tell God that everything you thought was yours now belongs to Him.

This process will take a few minutes for some and a few months for others! Trust God and let it go. Suddenly what you thought was yours is not yours anymore. Fear will dissipate. Freedom and joy will begin to creep into the places where fear hid. God will take care of it!

Chapter 3:
What is Money?
(You Might Be Surprised)

"Kids are not the same these days – in my day it was different! We understood the value of money!"

There are people in every generation who make statements such as these. These statements are probably true. Most children these days have no idea what money is.

In the current generation many kids rack up three-hundred dollar cell phone bills (or more!) and have no idea what allows that to take place or where the hundreds of dollars come from. The use of a cell phone is no different then the air kids breathe as far as they are concerned. Similarly, money is often just air to them. They know that when they want to go shopping for the latest trendy clothes, they need more air.

Unfortunately many parents foolishly hand out the "green air" like it is candy. This is due in part to the reality that most adults do not know what money is, either. Think of it this way: if I pulled a dollar out of my wallet and asked people what it was, their answer would be simple enough: "It is money." It may be called money but what I will address in this chapter is where the real value is coming from. A dollar bill is just a green and grey piece of paper. In many people's minds it has become a right to have it. If they do not have any they think someone should give them some.

Theft

One way to better explain the true definition of money is to talk about theft. Stealing is something that makes my blood boil. People who premeditate a theft have no idea what they are stealing. Even the most immoral thieves might think twice if they really knew what they were stealing. Thieves often justify their actions by thinking they are stealing someone else's unneeded abundance.

I know a little something about unneeded abundance. One afternoon my wife Laura startled me with an observation: "We have fourteen televisions." I responded, "No we don't, that is ridiculous." So she proceeded to show me up by listing off all of the appliances and monitors which serve that purpose. She counted them off and she was right. "One in the family room, one in the living room, one in the bedroom, two in your office, one in my office, two in the motor home, one in your car, one in my car, one we use outside near the outdoor kitchen, one you use for business when you travel and two we take for the kids when we go out to eat."

One of my passions is watching football. I love to multi-task and track several football games simultaneously. If you do not like football you would hate my place. If you came over to my house during football season you would see several TV's on all at the same time. It might seem chaotic and unmanageable to you but I love it and I do not want to miss a great play. I do not need fourteen TV's. Maybe I should have asked God if it was okay for us to have another TV before it got up to fourteen. However, that is not the point I am trying to illustrate. My point is this: if someone breaks into a home in the neighborhood and steals a television, the detective would of course ask, "What was taken?" The reply might be, "The television." Or in my case, more than one. But that is not what was taken! We need to understand what money is to know what was truly taken.

The "have-nots" often rationalize that the "haves" should give to them because that would only be fair. After all, air is free so if someone has fourteen televisions that is not fair. The "have-nots" think the "haves" are lucky. The "have-nots" think this way because they do not know what money is or where it comes from.

We have all heard the cliché that "time is money." That is true to a degree. It depends on what time is spent on. Time is not money, but instead it is a resource. If I spend a couple hours on the couch watching sitcoms, that has nothing to do with money.

I learned at the age of ten what money is: **money is labor.** My home and the televisions in it are labor. My stocks, real estate investments and businesses are pooled labor. When someone steals, that person is taking another's time spent laboring. That is why stealing infuriates me. I buy, sell, spend, and organize labor in order to store up more in God's account (remember, it does not belong to me). Labor is wealth. Labor is money.

Mowing Lawns, Skateboarding, and Labor

When I was ten I would mow lawns. It took me about two hours back then because the lawns were big and I had to trim the edges with those frustrating little scissor things. We did not have electric or gas powered weed whackers. I got paid $3 for mowing a lawn. After putting thirty cents in the Sunday school basket I would take the money and put it in a jar I kept on my dresser. I knew it was not just pieces of green paper stored in that jar. It was labor – my labor stored in the form of paper. If I wanted a new bike that cost $30 I had to spend my labor mowing eleven lawns for the bike. (I had to mow ten lawns for the bike and one for God's return on His investment.) The bike's cost had nothing to do with dollars. The cost was the time I spent laboring and more importantly what I produced. Labor that produces nothing is worthless. Instead of grasping this concept, the generation of children and teens today think the bike costs three hundred one-dollar bills – and the dollar bills might as well be air.

It did not take me long to realize that I did not want to be limited to my own time laboring. God has gifted me in leadership, management, and business. My mother, LaVon, saw this in me at an early age. She often tells a story that she finds very humorous. The story she tells goes like this:

> Three of Steve's friends came over to the house after school one day because they wanted Steve to go skateboarding with them. I told Steve he couldn't go anywhere until he swept the driveway, picked up the walnuts and raked the leaves. When I came back out of the house Steve had one of his friends sweeping the driveway, one picking up walnuts and one raking the leaves. He moved from friend to friend making sure each chore was done correctly but he didn't do any of the chores himself. He came into the house in a very short period of time and said, "I've got the chores done. May I go skateboarding now?"

What my mother didn't know was that my friends stopped by my house because they needed a fourth person to race catamarans. I convinced my friends that if we got organized we could have the chores done in twenty minutes and we could all pair up and make catamarans as we skateboarded down a hill. They thought that was a good idea so I organized their labor and managed them in doing my chores. I did not manipulate my friends. We all got what we wanted. All I did was harness labor so we could all spend it on what we wanted which was skateboarding. My guess is those three friends thirty years later are still spending their labor in the same manner. They give a portion of their labor to someone else and are limited to their own labor. They are employees and so their labor is harnessed by someone other than themselves.

Crawdads and Movies

Let me illustrate the concept in a different way. I live near Lake Tahoe and one activity my family enjoys is spending time on the lake boating and swimming. One weekend my family and I spent time up at the lake with my parents and siblings. The kids were having fun swimming and my nephew Riley wanted to borrow my niece Lindsey's goggles so he could catch crawdads. Lindsey was in tears because she thought her cousin Riley would lose her goggles and she did not want to let him use them. Remember, the goggles equal labor just like a television equals labor. Try to see the goggles as representing stored labor just like I looked at the bike when I was ten. I saw this as a perfect time for a business lesson.

Riley had $20 my sister Rene gave him, which can be thought of as twenty units of labor. First, I pulled Riley aside and asked him if he would pay Lindsey two dollars (two units of labor) for the use of her goggles. He replied, "Yes, I just want to catch crawdads." I said "Okay I think I can get the goggles for you." I then pulled Lindsey aside and asked her if she would rent Riley her goggles for two dollars. She refused. "No," she said, "he will lose them." I bargained with her. "Riley will give you a $20 deposit to hold until he brings the goggles back. If he loses them you will be able to buy ten new pairs of goggles." Lindsey understood. She took Riley's $20 and gave him the goggles.

Let me say this: children will catch on very fast if parents give them real life lessons. If parents do not understand real life finance they will not be able to teach their children. When parents understand finances these lessons are very simple and even fun.

My nephew and niece are perfect examples. Riley came back with five dollars after he caught crawdads. I asked him where he got the five bucks. He answered, "I sold the trout we caught earlier today to some people in the campground." Riley then boiled the crawdads and advertised to campers, "If anyone wants a crawdad they are one dollar each." He was simply trying to multiply his labor. A better description is he was profiting off his fun!

Lindsey started to catch on. She asked me if she could borrow a DVD from our motor home. She took the movie over to my parent's motor home and played it in their back bedroom. It amused me when I found out she was trying to charge all her cousins a $1 admission to watch the movie! Both Riley and Lindsey thought of ways to capture labor on their own. It took someone's labor to make the goggles. Riley and Lindsey both harnessed the labor it took to make the goggles for their own profit.

It's Never Too Early

Many say it is never too early to start talking to your kids about the dangers of drugs. Similarly, it is never too early to start teaching your children that money is not green air. Kids are notorious for always wanting something every time they enter a store. My daughter Kamryn is no different. She points to a toy and tells me she wants it. I ask her if she has any money. The answer is no, so I tell her she cannot buy it without money. In her little mind, it always ends up being my fault she does not have any money. I don't care if she is only four. It is not my fault she does not have any money to buy a toy. The sooner I teach my kids solid financial principles the better. If kids do not learn money is not green air then when they grow up someone else will always "be lucky" and it will be someone else's fault they do not have any money. Some people think this is a little harsh. My daughter can cry about not getting a toy when she's four, fourteen, or forty. Sooner or later she is going to cry about not having money to buy something. It is normal for a four year old to cry about this but not a forty year old. The problem is that many forty year olds cry because someone will not give them money!

My daughter and son love to come in my office and sit in the chairs on the other side of my desk. I shake their hands, give them a card and ask them if they are here for a job. My kids call these business meetings even though I'm their dad. They are both becoming very good negotiators. It is very adorable. They say things like "Let's make a deal" and "Let's make some money." Do not assume children cannot get it. Laura and I figure out all kinds of ways for them to make money or start businesses. If I tell Kamryn I will buy the picture she drew for $5, she says, "How about $6?"

Children can also learn to increase money by lending their allowance to their parents at a specified interest rate. Most kids do what most parents do: they get their allowance and spend it immediately. Let them learn these principles in your home as they would in real life as an adult. If children lend money make sure they understand there is a risk. Explain to them that they should obtain collateral just in case the loan is not paid back. If the loan is not paid back, take the child down to the pawn shop and sell the collateral or have a garage sale. It is important to let kids make mistakes. If they do not make mistakes they will not learn! If they cannot sell the collateral for at least the amount they loaned or if they don't have collateral, they will lose money.

One mistake parents make is to underestimate their children. Kids can count. Let them build confidence early so when they lose money they will not be fearful of losing more money. Let the setbacks occur. Remember the principle from the previous chapter: setbacks are good.

A Project With Your Children

Another great way for kids to learn about finances is to have them buy supplies with their allowance and make a product you have agreed to purchase from them. The same principles of making and losing money should apply.

If the supplies cost more than what they sell the product for they will lose money. If your children make money, show them the value of their labor: subtract the cost of supplies from the gross received from the sale of the product. Then divide the profit by the time it took to complete the project.

Let's say the supplies cost $10 and were sold for $20. It took two hours to complete the project so the value of the labor is $5 per hour. If your child hires a friend to make the product and pays the friend $2 per hour, your child just made $3 per hour off their investment and hired labor without spending their own labor or time. This child just bought and sold labor for a profit. These little games can get more detailed. The child might be required to pay taxes to the family to help pay for expenses.

One of my relatives has a daughter who likes to borrow money. But she rarely pays it back. That is because she thinks money is green air and credit cards are flat plastic. Why pay back a loan? Whoever she got the money from can just "breathe" more of it. Instead of perpetuating the pattern of loan-default-loan-default, my relative could simply hold three or four pairs of her designer jeans or her coveted MP3 player for collateral. Next time she wants to buy a pair of jeans for $70 he could hold those jeans until she gives him $85. This is the same effect of a credit card. She would learn fast that credit cards are not flat plastic and money is not air.

The bottom line is this: I believe parents should teach their children to stop thinking of ways they can get others to *give* them money and start thinking of ways they can *earn* money. If everyone looked for ways to get others to hand them labor it would just be a matter of time until no one would be performing labor and there would be none to give. If nothing is produced, there is nothing to give.

Chapter 4: Understanding Labor

In the last chapter I discussed the principles of money and labor. But what is labor really? What is time worth? We all have so much of it in this lifetime. Here is a harder question: what is time worth spent for God? Is it minimum wage, $5,000 an hour or somewhere in-between?

In order to build great wealth for God it is not only important to understand what money is but also to understand the value of labor. People who control wealth understand labor. I would guess that 50% of all people who are employees do not understand labor. Even employees who understand how money relates to labor do not truly understand labor.

There is a big difference between *need* and the value of labor. Many employees do not understand this distinction. Need and value are two different things. Most employees think *need* is the value of their labor.

Case Study 1: Professional Basketball

People think if Michael Jordan made $40,000,000 a year to play basketball he was being paid "way too much" because he did not need anywhere near that much money just to "play a game." Do you think the owner of the Chicago Bulls was making a huge mistake? Did he accidentally add a few zeros to Jordan's salary? Or did he know what he was doing? I believe the owner of the team knew that $40 million was the value of Jordan's labor, and more importantly, he profited off of that labor. Michael Jordan is his own economy. When he played basketball tens of thousands of people came to watch him. Fans had dinner at a local restaurant near the stadium, bought a Michael Jordan jersey and bought refreshments at the game. Vendors and service providers made more money in Chicago (including the owner of the Bulls) because of Michael Jordan.

In fact, if anyone got ripped off it was Michael Jordan! A lot of businesses made money because of him. As a matter of fact, when he played in other cities those cities should have paid him too.

Case Study 2: Professional Tiddlywinks

Let's say, for example, that I play tiddlywinks. Let's say that I play really well. If I am the only person in the world who knows how to play tiddlywinks and every person in the world wants to watch me play on Super Tiddlywinks Sunday, how much is my tiddlywinks labor worth? How much will advertisers pay to air their ads during the game? It will be millions per minute on live television world-wide. How much money will the network airing the game make? How much is my labor worth? How much will the network pay me? What if it is not one hundred million? I could say "I don't feel like playing tiddlywinks." People who control a lot of wealth understand labor and its value.

Case Study 3: The Trades

I have respect for people in the trades, and I know people who do great work and are paid well. But there are also people who hold signs on a road construction site who think they should be paid $20 per hour because they need to make that much money to support their families. I am not trying to offend people in this line of work, but remember, anyone can hold a sign. This is a simple supply and demand principle. The easier the task, the more people can do it. Tasks which are very hard, few people can do.

Let me say this another way: *an employee's needs have nothing to do with the value of their labor*. The higher the supply and lower the demand, the lower the value. The supply of dirt on this earth is very big and the demand is very small. The supply of people who are able to hold a sign is very big and the demand is very small. Many people have problems because they think money is green air and they do not understand the value of labor.

Here is another truth: hard work has no value. This statement is very shocking to most people. Hard work has no value! I have started many businesses and can say that I understand this – but most employees I have hired do not understand it. Hard work is inherently good. Hard work is a great work ethic to live by and is very important. Hard work can produce results. But it is the *production* that has value – not the hard work.

I have had numerous employees sit in my office and tell me I should pay them more because of their hard work and all that they are doing. My response has been, "How much do you think I should pay you to work as hard as you can eight hours a day digging a ditch behind our health club?" The correct answer is nothing. Most people just cannot get this. They do not understand that it does not matter how hard they work digging a ditch behind my club because the ditch has no value to me.

When I opened a health club in 1995 a man came in for an interview. I asked him what type of position he was looking for. He said he wanted the job of walking around and talking to members. Wow what a great job! I would have come up with something much better like the job where you hold a hat out and everyone tries to throw gold into it!

Calling the Bluff

In my career I have seen some very silly personal views of the value of labor that have really baffled me. Here is a real life example that will demonstrate the reality of labor supply and demand.

I recently flew back East to help a club near Philadelphia. This is a club that had been visited by many consultants in the preceding two years and wanted nothing to do with the management.

I went back for a week toward the end of February and took an assistant manager with me. We arrived in what they call a "snow storm" but it was more like ice cubes falling out of the sky! One of the first things I received was a notice from the electric company stating that the electricity was going to be shut off in two days. We started selling memberships and got the electric bill paid along with many other bills that were past due.

This club grossed $72,000 in January. Everyone in the health club business knows that January is always the best month of the year. The club was in critical shape. All of the gauges were blinking red and the owners of this club were about to lose hundreds of thousands of dollars including their homes. This business was in desperate condition.

We helped them turn it around and the club began grossing between two and five thousand dollars a day. Our first full month, which was March, this club grossed over $112,000.

Understanding the value of labor is like playing poker when you get to see your opponent's hand. The next time I talked to the president of the company I had a good understanding of where this business was. It had $400,000 in debt and there was no way it would make it without solid leadership and skilled human resources in the club.

I told the president we could probably build the profit of the club up $500,000 per year in two years. I had enough time evaluating the situation to know this was possible. In return my group would get 51% and complete control of the club. I would get a guaranteed consulting agreement for 10 years. He balked. His response was, "We can always talk to that other management company."

Now, I like sales. That is what I do. So I used what is called a take away. It is not a trick but it does call the other persons bluff and establish value. I said, "That might be a good idea. You should probably do that. I will call the old manager and see if he will come back in if you want. I want to go play with my kids now." He panicked. His response was, "Wait, wait, wait... are you serious?" "Yes, there are thousands of clubs out there we can buy. This is not that good of a deal for us." I can do this because I do not care about the money. He continued: "Okay but what if you die? How will that affect the consulting agreement?" I responded, "Give it to my wife." I got the deal.

This may sound mean; it is not. If I was mean and selfish I would not have cared about the loss the current ownership was about to incur. I would not have cared about them losing their homes. What I would have done is called the landlord the first day I arrived and told him we were interested in renting the club. That way I would have had 100% of the business and no debt. I have an obligation to not let people take advantage of the skills God has given me. I work for God and should not let people rip Him off. Since I work for God that means I always strive to have His best interest in mind. I want more for Him while helping others. That is what I did. The president of the company has told me many times he thinks I'm the best in the business. Well, if he really thinks that, he got the deal of a lifetime!

Severance

The story did not end with rebuilding the business. Something happened that set me off and made me a little cross-eyed. One of the managers there wanted to talk about severance pay after he quit. I did not go off like I wanted to, thankfully. One of the current managers wanted a lot of money for all his work in the last year. I simply said, "We do not do severance" although I wanted to say a lot more. My comment was accepted.

What if my comment was not accepted? If what I said was not accepted, I would have simply started negotiations. Here is where I would have started: "Okay, if you give all your paychecks back, I will not ask you to pay for the $400,000 you lost the company due to your performance." Worthless labor is worthless. The previous manager's labor was beyond worthless. It was very expensive. This may sound a little harsh but it is a fact. The people running the club before we got there were very nice and likable. They were just trying to perform the wrong kind of work with their ability. Those people will be much better at something else.

My business priority is always the employees who helped me build my clubs. I try to put them before myself without being unfair to me or God. I cut them in on just about everything. My business philosophy is employees come first. But anyone working for someone else better make their employer money or expect to get fired. That is what is deserved. Anyone that does not like this common sense should start their own business.

Chapter 5: Poor vs. Wealthy: A Mindset

I spoke about how quickly children learn and understand the concepts of money, labor and value. Unfortunately, many adults understand money, labor and supply and demand less than children! These concepts are often taught poorly or not at all in our schools or churches. I believe it is time for the church to take the lead in managing God's wealth instead of making excuses about wealth or tainting it with guilt.

Motive

There are two extremes that I have observed in the church. One is that if a Christ-follower does not have or does not control great wealth, that believer is doing something wrong and should claim his or her right to wealth. Please note the words I have emphasized in the following passage:

> What causes fights and quarrels among you? Don't they come from your desires that battle within you? You want something but don't get it. You kill and covet, but you cannot have what you want. You quarrel and fight. You do not have, because you do not ask God. **When you ask, you do not receive, because you ask with wrong motives, that you may spend what you get on your pleasures"** (James 4:1-3, emphasis added).

Let me emphasize something again: Motive! Motive! Motive! Our motives must be God's motives. Our purpose must be God's purpose. We cannot fool God. God knows our motives. God's first priority is our spiritual health. Having a lot of money can be very dangerous and bring us great ruin personally and professionally.

While writing this book I have done a lot of soul searching, a lot of research, and asked a lot of questions of friends and family. I think I could manage a billion dollars for God. I think I am mature enough to do what God wants me to do with it. Two of the questions I have asked are, "Do you think I could handle a billion dollars and do you think I would do what God wants me to do with it?" The response I get is, "Yes, I think you could." My next question is, "Then how come I do not have it?" One verse that might help explain the answer to that question is found in the book of Job: *"God's voice thunders in marvelous ways; He does great things beyond our understanding"* (Job 37:5).

The other extreme in the church is that money is bad and people who have a lot of it are not putting God first. They are selfish and greedy. I disagree with both extremes.

I do think people who build wealth and people who do not have two completely different mindsets as a general rule. Please bear with me while I generalize. I admit these generalizations are not always the case, but I have observed them enough to see trends in how people think and act.

The "have-nots" tend to think money is green air. I have addressed this in previous chapters. In other words, they don't understand the value behind money. Since they think money is green air they resent the "haves" because they have hogged up all the air. The "haves" should leave some for others. The "haves" are often described as greedy and selfish. The "haves" are often accused of exploiting the poor when in actuality it is the poor who often exploit themselves. The poor think all sweat is equal. People who build wealth know it is not. The value of labor is equal to what it produces. If labor does not produce value it is as worthless as a ditch in the back of my health club.

If someone does or does not have money there is a reason. People without money are tempted to blame those with money because they are "hoarding it all." It is also popular to blame the government for not refereeing fairly. The government is letting the "haves" breathe up all the green air. That's just not fair. Where is Robin Hood when you need him? The poor think the government should take care of them. The "haves" do not. The poor often look at how others have stolen their fair share of air instead of looking at their own misconceptions of wealth.

It just could be that the "have-nots" have a different perspective then the "haves." The "have-nots" tend to be takers while the "haves" are givers. The "have-nots" might look for ways to have money given to them while the "haves" instead look for ways to generate income. The "have-nots" look to people to take care of them. The "haves" (that truly have) look to God. The "have-nots" are tempted to hoard the little they have and the "haves" often let it go.

Trends

Have's

givers

look for ways to generate income

look to God to take care of them

often let their wealth go

Have Not's

Think all sweat is equal

Blame the "have's"

Blame the government

Expect the government to take care of them

Look for ways for money to be given to them

Look for people to take care of them

Hoard what they have

Look for *yourself* in the trends I have described. Where do you fit? Do you ever find yourself tempted to look for ways for money to be given to you instead of looking for ways to generate income?

Examine yourself! People with the "poor" mentality must first examine themselves and evaluate if there is something they are or are not doing that is causing their situation. The people with the "poor" mentality must stop finding excuses why someone else made them poor and is keeping them that way. No one makes someone else poor. If someone is poor it is not another's fault. At this point you as a reader might be thinking of situations where one person can make or has made another poor. Anyone thinking this way has the "poor" mentality! The "haves" don't think like this. No one can make me poor – especially since God has plans to prosper me. People that generate wealth think of ways to produce value, not take it or have it given to them.

Charity

Some forms of charity are very valuable to society. But giving to someone with the "poor" mentality who is constantly holding their hand out is detrimental. All this does is motivate the person with their hand out to keep it there. This is along the same lines as giving children money whenever they ask for it. People with a poor mindset must first *recognize it* and then *change* their paradigm.

People with a wealthy mindset understand a bigger picture, have less fear and get a bigger bang from their own labor and others.

Entrepreneurs

The people who live in the most expensive 1% of homes and make the most money are not doctors or lawyers; they are entrepreneurs, business people and investors who understand labor. (A doctor or lawyer could also be a good entrepreneur or business person but not always.) Good entrepreneurs are experts at buying, selling and spending labor whether that is in the form of creating businesses, investing in stocks or buying commodities. Entrepreneurs also create wealth and labor through *ideas*.

When a lawyer goes on vacation he makes nothing. When he sleeps at night he makes nothing. Anyone who earns income only through their own labor is limited. It does not matter how much someone makes per hour if the income only comes from their own labor. A good entrepreneur will make more money than a doctor will make in a lifetime before the doctor gets out of school! When Bill Gates goes to sleep at night, he wakes up millions of dollars richer. He is selling products to people every second of the day through the labor and ideas he has harnessed.

Chapter 6: Wealth Principles

People in the United States really do not know how incredibly wealthy this country is. They also do not understand why, and I think one of the primary reasons we are wealthy is due to our foreign policy decisions as they relate to the nation of Israel.

Spirituality

First let's look at some of the spiritual reasons this country has great wealth:

> *"I will make you into a great nation and I will bless you; I will make your name great, and you will be a blessing. I will bless those who bless you, and whoever curses you I will curse; and all peoples on earth will be blessed through you"* (Genesis 12:2-3).

> *"God brought them out of Egypt; they have the strength of a wild ox. They devour hostile nations and break their bones in pieces; with their arrows they pierce them. Like a lion they crouch and lie down, like a lioness—who dares to rouse them? "May those who bless you be blessed and those who curse you be cursed!"* (Numbers 24:8-9)

These passages are talking about Abraham and his descendents (which is the nation of Israel). I am not one to sugar coat things and I do not make the rules. Nations and peoples who hate Israel hate God. Nations which curse Israel are cursed. It is that simple and that obvious. I am not trying to make friends with this comment. It is the truth. God's Word is factual. Anyone who does not believe this is unable or unwilling to see the truth.

One reason the United States is blessed is because it blesses and supports Israel. As I write this, terrorist groups are attacking Israel. "Who dares to rouse them?" Israel is proceeding to turn the neighboring countries into a glass factory. Other countries might be next. "They are breaking bones into pieces." Countries that oppose Israel will have no recourse to God's wrath. Some countries are condemning Israel. That is an arrogant fool's mistake. If the United States ever does this it is time to hide. President Bush is blaming terrorist groups and at the same time supporting Israel's actions. This is a wise, biblical choice. The United States stood alone in vetoing a U.N. resolution telling Israel to stop their attacks. Some countries have threatened Israel. This is the equivalent of telling God you are going to throw a rock at Him.

Generosity

Another reason this country has wealth is because it gives.

> *"Give, and it will be given to you. A good measure, pressed down, shaken together and running over, will be poured into your lap. For with the measure you use, it will be measured to you"* (Luke 6:38).

This principle applies both to individuals as well as to groups or nations. The United States probably gives more to other countries than any nation in the history of the world. Other countries are quick to hold their hands out for U.S. aid and sometimes complain if it is not as much as they want. Many countries hate the United States because they think the United States gobbles up all the green air. Many poor countries do not even say "thank you" for our aid because they think the United States *owes* them aid. (After all, the United States is hogging all the wealth.) Poor countries and poor people need to lose the poor mentality and change their paradigm. This might sound harsh but there is a reason for everything, which I explained in the previous chapter. One of the pastors at our church asked me before a service if I was trying to give everything away.

Chuckling, I said, "No, I'm just really selfish and a very wise investor." His smile told me he could not argue with the wise investor part of my statement.

Harnessing Labor

Another reason the United States is wealthy is because it has harnessed the labor of other countries. Successful businesses in this country understand labor and its value.

The Nike Corporation is commonly criticized because they pay people fifty cents an hour in other countries to put glue on a shoe. The shoe glue laborers in this country do not think that is fair because they need $20 an hour to take care of their families. This is the "poor" mentality. These people do not understand what money is, the value of labor or supply and demand. The value of labor is not equal to *need* or *want*.

People can buy a shirt at Wal-Mart for $4. I never hear anyone complain about this. All I hear is complaints about how selfish Wal-Mart is and how they exploit others. The reality is that because Wal-Mart sells shirts for $4, many people in this country have five shirts instead of one.

People with the "poor" mentality do not understand why they cannot get paid $20 per hour, buy shirts for $4 and still keep their jobs. People with a "poor" mentality think they should have five cakes and eat ten.

In order to build and manage great wealth for God it is helpful to understand what money really is and why some individuals and countries control massive amounts of it. If an individual looks at a dollar as money or a piece of paper that can buy things, that individual will be at a disadvantage when it comes to building substantial wealth.

There are three major reasons that our country enjoys such unprecedented wealth: policies which support scriptural principles, generosity, and our ability to harness labor both here and abroad.

What about us as individuals? How can we harness labor and use a better understanding of wealth to build our resources and give them all to God? In the next few chapters I will detail some specifics which will equip you to harness labor and wealth and build capital for you and others.

PART II
Managing Money

Chapter 7: Developing a Personal Budget

The word "budget" is one of the scariest words in the English language. Many people do not have a budget either because they do not have the discipline that it requires or because they really do not want to know where their money is being spent.

A personal budget is something that many people do not have and probably do not understand. I thought it was normal for every family to have one because my dad always had one and talked about it all the time. Now that I'm grown, I realize personal budgets are probably rare. I think many people do not even balance their checkbook because they do not even know how! I do not think God is going to trust great wealth to people lacking this ability or discipline. Simply put, without a budget finances cannot be managed.

Many people balance their checkbooks by calling the bank and asking what their balance is. I have known business owners who do this. They are not in business anymore.

A basic understanding of math is needed to create a budget. Fortunately, there is more than one strategy that can be used. One key to a budget is to have the discipline to follow it. Another key is to live below your means. This means the money coming in each month is more than what is needed or spent each month. The bigger the difference between the money coming in and money going out will determine the quality of your budget and how well you are able to live below your means. It also means that God's *principle* is growing faster each month. The principle is net worth.

Sample Budget

The following budget is based on a monthly income of $5,000 for a family of four. It is structured so that a family living on this budget will be living below their means.

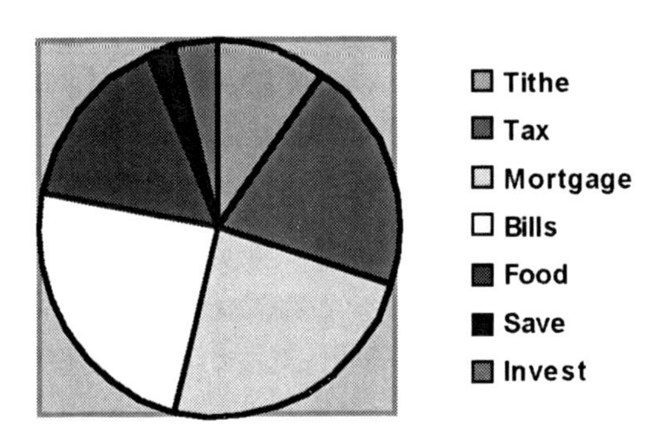

Tithe = 500

Tax = 1,000

Mortgage = 1,200

Bills = 1,200

Food = 800

Savings = 100

Investments = 200

Diligently tithing will increase the monthly income. The tithe is the most important payment made each month. I will discuss this in greater detail in a subsequent chapter.

The tax liability is estimated high but the excess at the end of the year can be shifted into savings or investments.

The mortgage payment will be high or low depending on the area of the country.

The bills line represents basic household bills such as electricity, gasoline and telephone. It also includes clothing and possibly a car payment with insurance. $1,200 is a low amount but it is doable.

The food allotment is not extravagant but this can be done. Most likely we have all lived on less than this at one time or another. When I was in college my budget was $350 a month and I ate well enough.

The $100 a month savings allotment is a cushion. As this builds, it will be available for emergencies and shifting into God's opportunities as He makes you aware of them.

The investment portion of the budget will grow. It is important to maintain discipline when investing.

Some keys to operating with a small budget is to maintain discipline, be patient, stay out of debt, and add to the tithe, offerings, savings and investments as the income grows. Do not increase the standard of living to the same degree of the growth. If the income goes up 10%, do not by any means increase the standard of living 10%. Increase it 3 to 5%! This takes a lot of discipline, particularly with the speed of technological development and how quickly technology becomes out of date. It is okay to be rewarded once in a while but stay well within the specified budget. Let God's principle grow. This is being a good steward.

It is okay to use credit cards as long as the whole principle balance is paid off every month. In other words, do not carry a balance. Do not spend money that is not there! If an item cannot be paid for completely, don't buy it!

What to Wear: The Standard of Living Dilemma

What kind of car should we drive? What kind of clothes should we wear? These are difficult questions without easy answers. These questions are worth wrestling through and praying through. These are questions worth asking and all too often people just get what they feel like without giving it much thought at all.

As a Christ-follower it is important to remember that you represent Christ. All believers are part of the body of Christ. We all have different roles. If two different believers with $100,000,000 both drive Rolls Royce's, that will not witness to as many people as if one lives in a mobile home and drives a Pinto. Both are witnesses for God in different ways and it is easy for me to see how both represent Christ.

I think what to wear and what to drive should be taken very seriously and most importantly should be led by God's Spirit.

I ask myself some hard questions when making these decisions:

Do I want this or does God want this?

How does this make God look?

How does this represent God?

Am I honoring God?

I commit my decisions to Him and then trust Him. This is what I would challenge you to do. I commit all my decisions to Him every day, whether they are related to purchases or something else. If you do this, as I have done, you will not find yourself wringing your hands or making a big deal over whether it is wrong to have 14 televisions.

All we can do is trust that these decisions will benefit God. Each Christian should trust God and not judge themselves or each other too much. Every individual and couple needs to discover what their standard of living should be based on a variety of factors. Over time my wife and I have found a comfortable middle ground and do not judge people who live more extravagantly or less extravagantly than we do.

I would call myself a middle of the road kind of guy. I do not wear a $50,000 watch but I usually do not wear watches under $2,000 either when I am in public. I do wear a $50 watch when I am hanging out at home because that is what I prefer! I don't drive a Bentley but I don't drive a Honda either. My wife really wants a Toyota van for her next car, but if she wanted a BMW, either would be fine with me. I usually wear custom suits but I prefer that they not cost more than $2,500.

In all actuality, I'm a jeans and t-shirt kind of guy; that's what I prefer. We live in what we consider a very nice home but it sure is not the nicest home in town. But it is in a nice neighborhood and we feel very blessed. Some people with a lot of money would probably consider it a dump but our home is used for God's glory! Some people probably drool over our home. Again, people on both sides tend to judge and we try to steer clear of that attitude. My wife likes to shop at very inexpensive clothing stores for herself but usually buys the kids what I would consider expensive clothes. I usually do not buy low-priced clothes for myself, however, because I feel it disrespects God and does not represent Him well. I like to buy my wife nice things because I think it honors her and God. I have tremendous respect for my wife and could not ask for a better mother for our children. Her birthday and Christmas presents are usually things like a swing set for the kids. I do not think I will ever be able to get her to stop shopping at low-end clothing stores any time soon, but don't get me wrong, I have been able to twist her arm hard enough a few times to get her into some fine clothing!

I write about these personal matters because I want you to get a feel for how I go about making these kinds of decisions and because I think it is very important to acknowledge God in how we present ourselves for His glory. What He wants is most important, not what we want. If we commit every decision to Him, He will direct our path. I really believe that these small decisions help to contribute to what is very exciting: giving to God's work. Giving to God's work is an incredible rush!

Chapter 8: Being a Steward of God's Resources

God wants us to be a good steward of His resources. God gives us many different types of gifts to serve Him.

> *"Do not neglect your gift, which was given you through a prophetic message when the body of elders laid their hands on you"* (1 Timothy 4:14).

> *"For this reason I remind you to fan into flame the gift of God, which is in you through the laying on of my hands"* (2 Timothy 1:6).

These two passages likely address a spiritual gift, but the principle is there that God gives us many talents and gifts to be used for Him.

This is how it works: when we turn our life over to Christ we become His servant. We are beyond servants, though, in the sense that we are adopted as one of God's children. Servants don't own anything but they are taken care of by their master. As a servant of God we should do everything to the best of our ability for Him because we love Him.

Got Talent?

Most people are good at some type of job. What are you good at doing? Jesus told a great story that helps illustrate how important it is to invest your talents for God's benefit:

> *"Again, it will be like a man going on a journey, who called his servants and entrusted his property to them. To one he gave five talents of money, to another two talents, and to another one talent, each according to his ability. Then he went on his journey. The man who*

had received the five talents went at once and put his money to work and gained five more. So also, the one with the two talents gained two more. But the man who had received the one talent went off, dug a hole in the ground and hid his master's money.

"After a long time the master of those servants returned and settled accounts with them. The man who had received the five talents brought the other five. 'Master,' he said, 'you entrusted me with five talents. See, I have gained five more.'

"His master replied, 'Well done, good and faithful servant! You have been faithful with a few things; I will put you in charge of many things. Come and share your master's happiness!'

"The man with the two talents also came. 'Master,' he said, 'you entrusted me with two talents; see, I have gained two more.'

"His master replied, 'Well done, good and faithful servant! You have been faithful with a few things; I will put you in charge of many things. Come and share your master's happiness!'

"Then the man who had received the one talent came. 'Master,' he said, 'I knew that you are a hard man, harvesting where you have not sown and gathering where you have not scattered seed. So I was afraid and went out and hid your talent in the ground. See, here is what belongs to you.'

"His master replied, 'you wicked, lazy servant! So you knew that I harvest where I have not sown and gather where I have not scattered seed? Well then, you should have

put my money on deposit with the bankers, so that when I returned I would have received it back with interest.'

"'Take the talent from him and give it to the one who has the ten talents. For everyone who has will be given more and he will have abundance. Whoever does not have, even what he has will be taken from him. And throw that worthless servant outside, into the darkness, where there will be weeping and gnashing of teeth'" (Matthew 25:14-30).

It is important to realize that a *talent* was worth approximately three months labor. The man, who represents Christ, entrusted his property to his servants. The property had a value in labor.

The first and second servants were praised because they increased the master's wealth. The master put them in charge of many things and invited them to share in his happiness. It is logical that these servants would receive a pay raise for managing their master's wealth so well – plus they would be given more to manage because of their ability to make wealth grow.

The master was angry with the last servant who had been given one talent. He expected this servant to grow his wealth even though he was only given one talent. This servant was called "wicked and lazy." I believe that fear prevented the servant from growing his master's wealth.

The master took the talent back and gave it to the first servant because he was good at managing wealth. Everyone that has will be given more. Even the little that someone does have will be taken away if wealth is not managed well. This will cause a downward spiral that will create a big hole and be difficult to climb out of. Remember, I did not say this, God did! I believe anyone who says God does not want us to build wealth is wrong, especially because of how the master reacted to the servants in this story that Jesus told.

(For further study see also Luke 19:11-26.)

Chapter 9:
Overcoming Fear

Experiencing fear about money is normal but can be very destructive. On the one hand, it is so normal that I hesitate to even write those words because fear is so universal to the human experience. But what concerns me most about fear in financial matters is how crippling fear can be when we deal with money and resources and how serious the consequences of fear can be.

It is time to give up being afraid! It is time to reject fear and pursue God's best for your life and for the money He has entrusted to you.

Do not be afraid to give big for God. Do not hold on to His money too tightly. It is exhilarating to put what God has entrusted to us in His hands.

There are not many things as exciting as trusting God and giving generously. God's word is powerful for those who can believe it:

"Remember this: Whoever sows sparingly will also reap sparingly, and whoever sows generously will also reap generously. Each man should give what he has decided in his heart to give, not reluctantly or under compulsion, for God loves a cheerful giver. And God is able to make all grace abound to you, so that in all things at all times, having all that you need, you will abound in every good work" (2 Corinthians 9:6-8).

"Now he who supplies seed to the sower and bread for food will also supply and increase your store of seed and will enlarge the harvest of your righteousness. You will be

made rich in every way so that you can be generous on every occasion, and through us your generosity will result in thanksgiving to God" (2 Corinthians 9:10-11).

The Antidote to Fear

For anyone having trouble believing this, or struggling with fear, let me make a suggestion. Read the above verses at least ten times every day. Make a recording of this passage and any others in this book or ones having to do with God's promises on this subject. Then play the recording every night as you sleep. Set the recording to play over and over. Another option is to get a compact disc player or MP3 player and set it to repeat. Get the Bible on CD and make the CD player repeat 2 Corinthians 9 all night. Doing this will change your life because I believe with my whole heart that God's Word is powerful. Read what this passage in Hebrews has to say about God's word:

"For the word of God is living and active. Sharper than any double-edged sword, it penetrates even to dividing soul and spirit, joints and marrow; it judges the thoughts and attitudes of the heart" (Hebrews 4:12).

This little exercise God has given me has changed my life. I have been hearing God's Word as I sleep for over half of my adult life. I'm not a scientist, but I'm going to say our spirits do not sleep. This means my spirit is hearing the Word of God all night.

Another verse that encourages me when it comes to hearing the message of God's Word is from Romans chapter ten:

"Consequently, faith comes from hearing the message, and the message is heard through the word of Christ" (Romans 10:17).

I have found it does not really matter what my carnal brain thinks. What matters is what my renewed spirit in Christ thinks.

Teaching Your Children

Unprovoked and without any arm-twisting whatsoever on my wife Laura's or my part, both of our children are believers. Our children have asked to receive Christ. Both of our kids have heard the Word at night since before they were born.

Recently we were at a renaissance fair with our kids. My son Dawson had a wooden sword and was looking for a fight. He challenged a man dressed as a pirate who was part of the fair. The exchange was really funny! The people involved in these renaissance fairs really play the part. After the conflict ended, we walked to the next exhibit. I was holding my daughter's hand but she did not want to walk where I was trying to take us. Have you ever tried to walk your child in one direction but your kid was trying to walk in a different direction? That is what was happening. It turns out she was pulling me back to the pirate. I finally gave in and we went back. Kamryn approached the pirate, pointed her finger right at his face and said, "You better watch out for Jesus." Apparently she took my son's duel with the pirate a little more seriously than everyone else. She was young but she knew her brother had an unfair advantage over the pirate because her brother knew Christ. Hearing the Word changes us!

I have seen some amazing things when I do not listen to the fears or doubts in my head and instead just act on the Word of God. When it comes to giving, the Nike commercials are right. "Just do it." Once you act on God's Word you will see how much faith is in your heart.

My wife and I recently attended a fundraiser for a Christian high school that God has put on our hearts. We bought a table at the event and invited a few couples to join us at our table for dinner.

The event finished with an auction to raise money for the school. My wife and I bid on a ranch-style barbeque for twelve people and a gourmet dinner for four. I did not know how much these items were going to cost but I did know God was going to buy them for Himself. At one point my own wife was bidding against me. The prices of these two items kept going higher and higher but God did buy both of them through my wife and me. A good friend of mine sitting next to me was looking at me like I had two heads. I leaned over and whispered in his ear, "I'm spending God's money like a drunken sailor." He burst into uncontrollable laughter. What was on my heart was how pleased God is when we sacrifice for others:

> *"And do not forget to do good and to share with others, for with such sacrifices God is pleased"* (Hebrews 13:16).

The next day I got a very nice e-mail from that friend thanking us for the evening and the experience. He finished his e-mail by writing, "I want to spend God's money like a drunken sailor, too." Not only is spending God's money well extremely fulfilling, but it is contagious too!

God takes care of us. He does not need us, but it is an honor to serve Him. Do not let fear or worry distract from serving Him. Remember, when we give money to God we are giving Him our time spent laboring. Whether we volunteer at the local church or give money, we are giving labor. It does not matter if a contribution to God's work is in the form of money or volunteer labor. God will multiply it. This is seed sown. Missionaries contribute their labor for God's work. That labor will multiply in ways we can't see. There is no way for us to know if a million dollars is greater or less than five hours spent witnessing. For now what matters is that we are giving generously of our time and resources to God and trusting Him for the results.

There are other resources than money that we can use to sow seed. Whatever resources God gives us, we should use them for His purpose. When we contribute money to God's work, we are really contributing labor. We are contributing value. When we give our time laboring to God, we are giving money. Money is labor. God will multiply that back to us in the form of green paper or more time to labor for Him. Read the following verses about finances that the Bible teaches and think about how you might want to spend your money differently:

> *"Each man should give what he has decided in his heart to give, not reluctantly or under compulsion, for God loves a cheerful giver"* (2 Corinthians 9:7).

> *"Therefore I tell you, do not worry about your life, what you will eat or drink; or about your body, what you will wear. Is not life more important than food, and the body more important than clothes? Look at the birds of the air; they do not sow or reap or store away in barns, and yet your heavenly Father feeds them. Are you not much more valuable than they? Who of you by worrying can add a single hour to his life?"*

> *"And why do you worry about clothes? See how the lilies of the field grow. They do not labor or spin. Yet I tell you that not even Solomon in all his splendor was dressed like one of these. If that is how God clothes the grass of the field, which is here today and tomorrow is thrown into the fire, will He not much more clothe you, O you of little faith? So do not worry, saying, 'What shall we eat?' or 'What shall we drink?' or 'What shall we wear?' For the pagans run after all these things, and your heavenly Father knows that you need them. But seek first His kingdom and His righteousness, and all these things will be given to you as well. Therefore do not worry about tomorrow, for tomorrow will worry about itself. Each day has enough trouble of its own"* (Matthew 6:25-34).

Fear does not come from God and it is a major deterrent to building wealth for Him. Many of the "have-nots" make excuses to hide their fear and disguise the fact that they are worshiping money. The "have-nots" accuse the "haves" of being greedy, selfish, money-loving and hoarding it. The less money the "have-not's" possess, the more they tend to cling to what they have. They might say things like "money is not important," but this is usually a lie. Many people say money is not important only because they are afraid to step out and take a chance on something that could make some money. We all have our prejudices on both sides when it comes to people with or without money. The "haves" often look down their noses at the fearful "have-nots" and the "have-nots" tear down the "haves" to disguise their fear.

Fearlessness

Many people are trapped in a job God does not want them in because of fear. They fear if they lose their job they will not be able to clothe or feed themselves or their families. It is fear and a lack of faith that suppresses so many people. It is devastating. God wants responsibility for taking care of us. I am not saying do not work. I am saying to work for God and be influenced by Him. If a bill is due in a week, do not worry about it. Do not worry but do not be irresponsible either.

For some people, worrying about something is "doing" something about it, and when they stop worrying about money they somehow feel *irresponsible*. If you struggle with this, put worry to death in your life. Live responsibly without worry. I will write it again: live responsibly without worry. You can do this!

When people have fears over money or not having enough, money controls them. When money controls someone it becomes a god to that person. What does having a lot or a little have to do with loving money? Do not think just because someone does not have money they don't love money. There are poor people who love and desire money – they just do not have any. Most believers who manage great wealth for God do not love money. That is why they can manage a lot of it.

We are all human. Money influences even the strongest Christians to one degree or another. We all do things for money. When money influences someone very little, they feel really good. People make financial decisions most days and think about financial situations constantly. These thoughts and decisions should be influenced by God. We all manage His wealth whether we recognize it or not. Fear and greed do not influence God, but they can certainly influence us, and if we are not careful, they can paralyze us into not doing anything significant for God.

Chapter 10: The Tithe: God's Return on Investment

You may already know that "tithe" is a word that means ten percent, and that many Christians use this giving percentage as a gauge or barometer as to whether they are really surrendering their lives and their finances to Christ's control. God often calls people to give far more than this, but nation-wide Christians, on average, give away about two percent of their money which is a tragedy on so many levels.

But even among those Christians who do give ten percent to their church there can still be a significant misconception about it. Many Christians believe that when money comes in, 10% belongs to God and the rest belongs to the individual or family. Many people say the tithe is God's portion of what He gives us. On the contrary, I believe *everything* God has put under my management is His – including the 90%. I am not the owner, I am the manager. The owner, God, expects a minimum of a 10% return on His investment. That is the tithe.

If God does not get a return on His investment He will put His investment somewhere else where He gets at least a 10% return. The tithe is given to the church that feeds you. For my family and me, we consider that to be two churches. We tithe to both of them and give offerings (gifts over and above a tithe) as God leads.

If God gets a 15% return on His investment without losing any principle, that is pretty good! If He gets a 25% return on His investment and His principle grows every month that is even better. Therefore as a manager it is wise to create a budget that provides for *an increase in principle* every month. This increased principle can earn more income for God. (Here principle = net worth.) It is best if the increase in principle increases your income.

Here is an example to help clarify. Let us say that you are struggling over whether or not to make a purchase of a swimming pool for your family. You alone need to come to terms with that purchase the same way that I come to terms with what I purchase for my family. But in terms of increasing principle, you will need to realize that buying the swimming pool will not increase your income. This does not mean, of course, that you should "not buy a swimming pool." You and God will know how you will use it and the kind of investment it will be in your family's physical and relational health. But it will not increase your income.

Is Tithing Optional?

One time, someone was talking to my wife about finances and the tithe. "If you do not have enough money to pay your tithe, it is okay. Just pay what you can." That sounds ridiculous to me, and is not what God says. He says to bring in the whole tithe. If we don't give the whole tithe we are robbing God:

> *"Will a man rob God? Yet you rob me. "But you ask, 'How do we rob you?' 'In tithes and offerings. You are under a curse—the whole nation of you—because you are robbing me. Bring the whole tithe into the storehouse, that there may be food in my house. Test me in this,' says the LORD Almighty, 'and see if I will not throw open the floodgates of heaven and pour out so much blessing that you will not have room enough for it. I will prevent pests from devouring your crops, and the vines in your fields will not cast their fruit,' says the LORD Almighty."* (Malachi 7:8-11).

I have been asked why some people who do not tithe – and are not Christians – have so much money. My response is that things are not always as they appear:

> *"A good man leaves an inheritance for his children's children, but a sinner's wealth is stored up for the righteous"* (Proverbs 13:22).

This verse indicates that non believers' wealth is just being stored up for the righteous.

One day I was showing my son how to play checkers. He got very frustrated when I moved the red checkers onto the black squares. Angrily, he moved the red checkers back onto the red squares. It did not make sense to him to put the red checkers on the black squares. It was logical to him to put the black checkers on the black squares and the red checkers on the red squares. In my son's mind, it was me who was wrong – but anyone who knows how to play checkers knows all the checkers go on the black squares.

I once asked a friend to tell me what he thought my wisdom and understanding was compared to my two-year-old son's on a scale of 1 to 10. He said it was a 9. In his mind it was not a 10 because my son can talk and understands basics. I then asked him what he thought God's wisdom and understanding was compared to mine on a scale of 1 to 10. He said 12. I agreed: "God's understanding of things is off the chart compared to mine."

> *"Trust in the LORD with all your heart and lean not on your own understanding; in all your ways acknowledge Him, and He will make your paths straight"* (Proverbs 3:4-6).

My young son would be wise not to lean on his own understanding of how to play checkers. I know how to play and he does not! So why do people think their own understanding is always correct and God should agree with it?

Why do people make up their own rules? If a person makes $1,000 per month and their bills are $950 per month, it makes perfect sense that this person "can not afford" a $100 tithe. But the fact is this person can not afford *not* to tithe. What is stopping the car, refrigerator, and washing machine from breaking down? Have you ever found a $20 bill in your pocket or on the ground or received a check in the mail you had no idea was coming? This does not even begin to account for all the things which could break down or stop working but somehow, miraculously, function well.

Why do we rationalize our silly fears by quoting scripture to explain why God says we do not have to tithe? "It's okay to give what you have if you do not have enough right?" Instead, why not just test God like He says to do with the tithe and trust Him. Any rationalization of why God would not want us to give the whole tithe is as foolish as trying to put the red checkers on the red squares. People often get frustrated with God because He will not let them put the red checkers on the red squares!

God wants at least a 10% return on His money. I like to invest assets where the return and risk are the best. If God does not get at least a 10% return on His money, He will invest it somewhere else. God is wise and will not make foolish investments. A wise investor does not want his principle reduced either. If an investor gives me a million dollars to manage and I give it all away, I will not be managing anything for long. I do not believe God puts wealth into our hands to give it all away.

Furthermore, God does not need me as a middle man. As a matter of fact, He doesn't need me at all! I need Him and it is an honor to serve Him. If He wanted what He has given me to manage somewhere else, He would have put it there in the first place. Imagine what the master would have said to the third servant if he gave the one talent away. The master was mad enough just because the servant did not make it grow.

God's expectation of a 10% return is a good marker for me. I do not invest in anything long term that I know will not yield at least a 10% return. If God expects at least a 10% return, why would I accept less when investing God's resources?

PART III
Investing Money

Chapter 11: Fuzzy Math

1 + 1 =?

Individuals and families sometimes struggle financially. This is also true for businesses and churches. Some churches struggle financially. Do you think our Father is turning to His Son and saying, "Oh no! What are we going to do? Our ABC church does not have any money! I sure hope all the people in our ABC church tithe this month!"

We know God does not act like that. So why should His servants? Christians serve the King of kings and the Lord of lords. He can make rocks rise up and praise Him. He can make bread fall out of the sky and make one fish feed thousands. He does not *need* our tithe. He is the ruler of everything. Our God is mightier than our little brains can comprehend. His ways are not our ways and "1 + 1" is whatever He wants it to be!

> *"For my thoughts are not your thoughts, neither are your ways my ways," declares the Lord"* (Isaiah 55:8).

If He leads us to give $5 above the tithe as an offering or $5,000,000, that is what we should do. God rewards obedience more than sacrifice:

> *"To do what is right and just is more acceptable to the Lord than sacrifice"* (Proverbs 21:3).

If I manage God's money well and make it grow, I will get paid well just like any money manager would. I am a servant of God. If I manage the talents He has given me well, He will be pleased and entrust more to me. If I waste or squander His resources why would God give me great wealth to manage?

I once asked a friend that was struggling financially if he thought he would do what God would want him to do with $100,000. "If God handed you $100,000 right now, what would you do with it?" The look on my friend's face was probably something similar to the look on the face of the rich young man Jesus asked to give all his money away and follow Him. I told my friend, "That is why God does not give you money." If we do not do what God wants us to do with money, we are doing the wrong thing with it. Why would God give us something we are going to do the wrong thing with? Why wouldn't God give me a trillion dollars if I did exactly what He wanted with it? He would.

Odds

There are no odds with God. The problem with us is that our little pea brains are always putting odds on things. It is just as easy for Him to raise someone from the dead as it is to fix my hangnail. It is just as easy for God to give me a trillion dollars as it is one dollar. It is not hard for God to believe He can give someone five dollars or ten trillion. The problem lies with us. It is hard for us to believe five dollars and ten trillion are the same for God.

I am reading a very inspiring book given to me by my pastor, John Jackson. I give John credit for knowing his flock well and knowing exactly what to feed them. The book is called "In a Pit with a Lion on a Snowy Day" written by Mark Batterson (Multnomah). In the book, Mark is challenging believers to be lion-chasers. Mark seems like the type of believer who chases down lions, kills them, chops them up into little pieces then eats them raw. I have never met this guy but I like him!

Mark really emphasizes things we all know but all too often forget. Our God is bigger than we can imagine. No matter how big we can imagine Him, we are still putting Him in a box much smaller than an atom. 1 + 1 is infinity with God. Our brains are not even capable of understanding infinity. We try, but in the end we cannot. We do, however, get ringside seats at watching God's math in action. It is awesome to see!

Case Study: Building a Church

I would like to start with a dilemma for you to think about. Decisions that are so obvious (using our logic) are not always the right choices. Apply your logic to two different choices:

1. Spend $15,000 in Africa. This $15,000 will build a church, a school, and a hospital. Tens of thousands of people will be saved.
2. Spend $15,000 on a new tile floor at the local church.

Now apply logic. Which is the better choice? If your answer was either of these, you are just guessing and only have a fifty percent chance of getting the right answer. The correct answer, which you may have figured out by now, is what God wants done with the money.

Let's build a scenario for the second choice and apply logic again. What if the new tile in the local church inspires a multi-millionaire to take the church seriously, and then he gets connected with God and ends up donating money to build one hundred churches in Africa? Now apply logic. Which is the better choice? The correct choice is, yet again, what God wants.

The moral of this lesson is to acknowledge God and not lean on our own understanding. If we lean on our own understanding we might put the red checkers on the red squares. It makes sense that the red should go on red but that might not be where God wants them!

Chapter 12: The True Cost of a Job

If you are an employee, you might enjoy the freedom from responsibility of running the business. There are wonderful benefits from spending a portion of your working life focusing on your particular position instead of having to track the important elements of every position in your workplace. However, employees must understand (1) what they are paying for, and (2) the risk of being an employee. I am not saying, "Do not be an employee." I am saying there are costs and risks that you should be aware of.

Enron employees found this out the hard way. Retired General Motors employees have to wonder how secure their retirement is. Security is a major issue for many of us and it is important to put trust in God first, not a big corporation.

People who are employees must (1) pay all the company bills, and then (2) pay rent. I will explain. Let's say a company has ten employees and the company profits $10,000 per month. Each employee gets a paycheck for $3,000 each month. Each employee got paid $3,000 per month but each employee's labor earned $4,000 per month. The first $1,000 each month is kept by the company in the form of profit to the company. In this example, an employee's labor has been harnessed. I call this "rent." This rent is paid after the employees pay all the company's bills with their labor. One owner cannot pay all of a company's bills by himself.

If I am a business owner, employees pay all my business bills and then pay me for the privilege of having a job. If the company loses $10,000 per month, I see this as the equivalent of paying the corporate rent with employee's personal credit cards. Think of it this way: employees are not required to pay the companies debt but individuals that rack up too much debt cannot pay for their credit cards either. They lose their credit cards and their purchasing power. Employees that work for companies that lose money lose their jobs. Working for a company that loses money is a big risk for an employee. There certainly is not much of a future being built. Remember what God says:

> *"For I know the plans I have for you," declares the LORD, "plans to prosper you and not to harm you, plans to give you hope and a future"* (Jeremiah 29:11).

Companies that want to make more money often lay off employees. If an employee does not produce up to the companies standards he or she is at risk of being fired.

The next thing an employee pays for is social security. I follow the laws of our country but often mock the idea of social security. First, "Social"? We live in a capitalistic society. This country was not founded on socialism. Next, "Security"? This is humorous. After corporate rent, about 7.5 percent of an employee's paycheck goes to social security. If an employee makes $80,000 a year, $6,000 goes to the government so they can spend it for me. Then even though they already spent it, they will "give it back" with interest when the employee is old and grey. Don't get me wrong. I am a big supporter of our government and follow its laws. That is God's way and His instructions. The key is to know the laws. Read what the Bible has to say about this:

> *"Everyone must submit himself to the governing authorities, for there is no authority except that which God has established. The authorities that exist have been established by God. Consequently, he who rebels against the authority is rebelling against what God has instituted, and those who do so will bring judgment on themselves. For rulers hold no terror for those who do right, but for those who do wrong. Do you want to be*

free from fear of the one in authority? Then do what is right and he will commend you. For he is God's servant to do you good. But if you do wrong, be afraid, for he does not bear the sword for nothing. He is God's servant, an agent of wrath to bring punishment on the wrongdoer. Therefore, it is necessary to submit to the authorities, not only because of possible punishment but also because of conscience. This is also why you pay taxes, for the authorities are God's servants, who give their full time to governing. Give everyone what you owe him: If you owe taxes, pay taxes; if revenue, then revenue; if respect, then respect; if honor, then honor" (Romans 13:1-7).

This is an important biblical principle for building wealth. It is wise to *follow God's instructions.* God does not say to pay more tax than what is owed. It is not wise for someone to pay more tax than he or she owes. Even the Internal Revenue Service will tell people not to do this and gives a refund when there is an overpayment. Many laws are written for the fearful and uniformed for their own protection. In a later chapter I will explain why social security is often not required. Robert Kiyosaki likes to point out that the rich play by a different set of rules. He is correct, even though they follow all the same laws.

Many of my businesses have been audited, as well as my personal financial affairs. The auditors I have dealt with have been very friendly and helpful. If you have followed the rules and done nothing wrong, you have nothing to fear. If you do something wrong, be afraid!

After social security is paid, the employee pays Medicare. This is about 1.45%. This is to help take care of an employee's medical needs after retirement.

Next the employee is allowed to subtract standard deductions or itemized deductions and exemptions from their income. The rest of the paycheck is subject to federal and state income tax. (Some states do not impose state income tax.)

When it is all said and done most employees receive very little of what their labor has really produced. Employees' jobs are not even close to as secure as a business owner's such as myself, and all employees should know what they are paying for and the risks of being an employee. Working at a job might have less responsibility and stress, but it is expensive and very risky.

Why Harness Labor

Now that I have tried to convince you that just working at a job is not only risky but also expensive, let me discuss the path I took that helped me determine why I should attempt to harness labor. I have started many businesses with very little or no money. The key has been to harness labor as a team not as an "owner with employees." What I call harnessing labor can also be described as "making your money work for you." I like to call it harnessing labor because that can also include making *someone else's* money work for me as well as them.

During college I worked in a health club making $4.50 an hour. If the owner of the health club would have provided opportunities for me I would probably still be working with him. My labor or sweat-equity was being transferred into someone else's labor account! My own labor was being stolen without an opportunity to build wealth in God's account. Because of this, after college I took a job in Palm Desert as a personal trainer working at a spa.

My new job in Palm Desert was with a large publicly held company and paid about twice as much as my previous job. I retained more of my own labor but this company was too big with too many rules and regulations to give me the opportunities I was looking for.

I soon saw that people would pay me $30 an hour to tell them what to eat and show them how to exercise in the Palm

Springs area. So, I soon started my own business as a personal trainer making $30 an hour. It wasn't long before I was able to quit my $10 an hour job at the spa! At this time it was the late 1980's and I was making pretty good money. I was able to invest some money and build a little wealth. (Let me emphasize *little*. It was only a few thousand dollars!)

Every year I would take a week or two off and take a trip to Lake Tahoe for a little fishing. I knew what I was doing – I was tapping into stored labor to pay for the trip. Not only was I spending labor I had stored up, I was not using any time laboring in order to build wealth. I knew I could be doing so much more. Just like when I was a young boy, I did not want to be limited by my own time spent laboring. I knew if I was going to increase my wealth building potential I had to find a way to harness more than my own labor and resources.

My dream at the time was to open a health club. Now, in order to maximize the success of a business it is important to find an area that has a need for the proposed business. In other words, the business should be placed where the demand for the business is *high* and the supply is *low*. I should mention this only applies to businesses that provide their products or services to a local population. It is also important to realize how globalization and technology will affect the business. (If a business has a plan to provide products or services internationally, for example, the variables of choosing a location would obviously be different.) In the case of an international business, such things as tax benefits, labor costs, and other business expenses should be considered.

I wanted to open a health club so I needed to find an area where the demand was high and the supply was low. I started doing my research and demographic studies in the early 90's.

First I had to do some research on the demand for health clubs. I found that 7% of the population would join a health club and that percentage was growing. Compare that to the data from 2006 which showed that 14% of the population would join a health club. And that percentage is still growing today.

I started looking at demographics in all the Western United States. At that time I pinpointed Carson City, Nevada which had a population density of 45,000 people and growing. At the time this town only had two health clubs. A third club did not sell memberships but charged a day fee for anyone that wanted to use their facility. Further research indicated that about 1,400 people in Carson City were members of a health club. If you know your math you know that seven percent of 45,000 is 3,150. That meant there were 1,750 potential members for a new health club in this town.

The existing 1,400 health club members in Carson City were all paying about $35 a month for their memberships. I developed a business plan with the assumption that we would sell memberships for $22 a month. After thoroughly investigating all other costs of operating a health club, my business plan indicated that a significant profit could be made by owning a health club in Carson City.

The next step was to acquire an investor to start the business – because I did not have any money. I will make a long story short here and just say we got an investor who invested an initial $79,000. About $20,000 of that initial investment was used and the rest was held in reserve. We started selling memberships in Carson City, Nevada while our building was being built. The initial investment was paid back in less than one year and that investor has made millions on his investment.

In 2002, one of our members asked me if I would be interested in buying a club in Elko, Nevada that was owned by one of his in-laws.

I took a trip out to Elko to look at the business. The owner was a very nice lady but she did not know much more about her business than where it was located. The club was just breaking even which was lucky considering how it was run.

After interviewing the owner I discovered she owned the building as well as the business. Her mortgage was about $5,000 per month. I proposed we would take over the business and rent the building from her for $12,000 per month. I knew the size of the building was about 12,000 square feet. This gave her an immediate positive cash flow. She was now able to retire which is what she wanted.

I split up the new business among some of our key employees and sent a staff out to Elko. We quickly tripled the revenue. In a couple years we put the business up for sale. I went back to the owner of the building and asked her if she was interested in selling the building. She said yes but thought the building was only worth about $300,000. I told her she could get $900,000 very easily. She was very excited and wanted to do it.

I found a young couple that wanted to get into the health club business. They bought the building for $900,000 and the business from us for $500,000. Everyone was overjoyed. This was a win-win-win. The owner of the building pocketed about $700,000. We pocketed $500,000, and the young couple got into their dream business for less than the value of the property.

This was not a bad return on our initial investment of nothing!

Using Borrowed Money

In many ways, banks are ridiculous. Banks do not really have money. They charge us to hold our money and then charge us again to borrow it. In doing so, the banks harness our labor. I became very frustrated with my bank. After many years in business it was still like pulling teeth to get my bank to loan me less money than I had in the bank. Banks borrow money from one person and lend it to another at a higher interest rate. After many years of being irritated by banks, I decided to look for ways to get in on the bank's game instead of just letting the bank use my money for their advantage.

Often when a person borrows money the lender benefits and the borrower does not. Remember my definition of money? Well, when money is borrowed, *labor* is borrowed. If labor is borrowed and does not produce anything, the labor must be paid back with the borrower's labor. Without getting too deep into sophisticated financial terms I will discuss the wise use of a lender's labor in very simple terms. Because understanding the cost of capital and the time value of money will go a long way in building wealth.

The first example I will use is one I have actually done, although I have changed the numbers to simplify the example. I borrowed $100,000 on my home equity line of credit then bought equipment that was leased to the health clubs I owned at the time. The $100,000 was borrowed at 7% interest-only. The lease I gave to the clubs was amortized over 5 years at 15%. At that interest rate, the total amount to be paid to me over five years would be $142,739, or $2,379 per month. In thirty-eighth months the $100,000 I borrowed would be paid back (if I put each of the payments I received against the debt). The last 22 payments I get to pocket. This means I would earn $52,338 in five years using the bank's labor. Of course, the labor really belongs to Tom, Dick and Harry who put their money in their checking and saving accounts.

Many people would say this is risky. Maybe, but I made a return of infinity %. Zero dollars invested earned $52,338. I like that risk-to-reward ratio. Yes, I had the risk of paying back the labor I borrowed from Tom, Dick, and Harry, but the equipment was collateralized and it did not cost me a dime. I also had inside information on the strength of the business I lent Tom, Dick, and Harry's labor to because I was consulting for the club.

Remember, Tom Dick and Harry put their money in the bank. I used the money when I borrowed money on my home equity line of credit.

Those of you who are wise in financial matters have already figured out that there is more to this example than meets the eye. That is what good accountants are for. The benefit to me is actually more than $52,338 because I get a *tax deduction* for the interest I pay on the loan. So, for the sake of example, if I am in the 35% tax bracket and pay $7,000 in interest the first year, I will pay $2,450 less on my taxes. In other words I get 35% back on the interest I pay each year. Furthermore, I also get to depreciate the equipment giving me even *greater* tax relief.

Let's vary the example a little bit. It is also possible that the equipment lease or note that is collateralized by the equipment could be sold immediately. The note could be sold, for example, for $120,000 to a third party. If that is the case, I would pay off the $100,000 debt on my line of credit and pocket $20,000.

This may sound quite complicated and it certainly can be. For most people this is not easy to understand, but I have tried to simplify the accounting to make it as understandable as possible. My main point is that if money is borrowed at 7% interest; make sure it is earning more than 7%! Can you guess one type of industry I like to buy stock in? Financials!

Big financial institutions and Wall Street are playing with labor. That labor belongs to most of the people reading this book. The more an individual understands money and labor the more that person will be able to build wealth for their (read: God's) account. This is harvesting where you have not sown and gathering where you have not scattered seed. This is like what the servant who buried the talent was referring to when describing the Master.

The Time-Value of Money

You have begun to learn the value of understanding the cost and value of capital, but now I would like to shift our attention to understanding the time-value of money. I want to go back to the example I shared previously about mowing lawns. When I was a boy I mowed lawns for $3. It took me 2 to 3 hours to mow a lawn. If I put that money under my mattress and kept it there until now it would be worth about 30 cents because of the cost of inflation. There is a formula to determine this but for the sake of simplicity I will just ask you to trust me on what the value of the $3 would be in today's dollars.

There is more than one reason for the devaluation of the money I earned so many years ago. For this example I used an average inflation rate of 3% annually to estimate the present value of the money I earned when I was a boy.

Technology is another factor that influences the value of money. Once again I will refer to money as labor. It took me two hours to earn $3 when I was a boy. Now it costs $30 for two men to groom my lawn in ten minutes. (They don't use those scissor things anymore!)

In terms of the time-value of money, if I invested $3 thirty years ago and it earned 8% every year it would be worth about $30. Interestingly, this is about the cost of mowing my lawn today. This may be a reason why the Master was angry with the servant that buried the talent.

Risk

When investing I believe it is crucial to evaluate the potential risk versus reward. It is one thing to read this on paper and think, "How basic!", s it is an entirely different thing to learn it from the "University of Life." I have made more failed investment decisions then successful ones! The key is that fortunately all the failed investments have had very little risk. In other words, the losses have been extremely small comparatively. Whatever you do, do not bet your first-born child on number seven at the roulette table. Make sure the odds are in your favor. If the odds are not in your favor then make sure the potential loss will be small while the upside potential is large. There is nothing wrong with swinging for the fence once in a while as long as it is not too costly – as long as the potential loss is small and the potential gain is large.

When you begin investing, develop a good strategy and philosophy that fits with your strengths – and stick with it. Build and develop that strategy and then know when to quit. Do not be tempted by the latest fad. Do not stick with a bad strategy or investment if it is not working. Continuously fine tune and stick with a good strategy for success. The most successful investors know when to cut their losses.

These *odds* concepts may seem a little contradictory when contrasted with other advice I have given, so let me give you a rule to go with everything written in this book. The rule is to always do what you think God is leading you to do. If God's choice is chosen, it will always be the right choice even if it doesn't appear that way in the short term. Remember, God is interested in shaping your character as well as shaping your resources for His benefit and glory.

Chapter 13:
Starting a Business

In my view, the best investment that can be made is buying or starting a business. I have bought businesses and started many more. I started a health club in 1994 then used the income to buy property and build a second. It was much more difficult to start a business back then compared to today. Technological advances make it easier and the increased wealth in this country has made venture capital abundant.

With a little research and a little imagination, online businesses can be started with a few hundred dollars, very little risk and great upside potential. Online malls can be created and merchandise can be drop-shipped. Many services can be provided online such as accounting and consulting. It just takes an idea, a plan and a little discipline. A business that builds good income can be sold for three to four times *EBITDA* (Earnings Before Interest Taxes Depreciation and Amortization) or more.

I will not get into the complicated details of the *EBITDA* formula, but in a nut-shell, when a business is bought using this formula it basically means the business is being bought debt-free at a certain number of times the earnings. I like this type of investment because it means if a business is bought at three times earning for $300,000, the business is earning $100,000 a year. That is a 33% annual return on the investment. It is very difficult if not impossible to make this type of return consistently in stocks or real estate. $300,000 may sound like a lot of money but not if money is pooled with other investors, borrowed or raised through venture capital. If $50,000 is invested and $250,000 is borrowed at 8% over 10 years, the payment on the loan would be about $36,500 annually. This is called *leveraging*.

A $50,000 investment will earn about $63,500 annually. Now the investment more than doubled in one year. This is return on invested capital. In addition, $17,000 the first year will be paid off on the loan. I have made this sound a little easier than it is but it certainly is not extremely difficult either. It takes detailed do-diligence and an understanding of finance. It can be accomplished by just about anyone without fear who is dedicated to learning and researching what it takes to do this. Fearful people will be tempted to bury their talent.

Growth Potential

Let's take the same example of putting $50,000 down to buy a business. If the business is operated more efficiently and improved the profit might go up to $110,000 the first year. Now the business could be sold for *four times EBITDA* because the business is showing growth potential. The selling price would be $440,000. The loan would be paid off at $233,000 and the initial investment of $50,000 returned. The one-year profit would be $157,000 from the sale of the business. Add in the $63,500 earned the first year and the profit is now $220,500. Again, I have simplified the numbers and left out the intricate details just to show the potential. The actual benefit is determined by the business skill and knowledge applied.

Real Estate

It should not take a genius to figure out the "real estate secrets" shared in infomercials and seminars are not secrets. If you think you can go buy real estate for pennies on the dollar because of the infomercial on cable, then be my guest and go ahead and try it. Real estate is a *commodity*. Money is made in real estate when it is bought while very few people want it. When everyone wants it, it is time to sell!

Although I prefer investing in businesses, I have built significant wealth through real estate. I must emphasize of course that this is only because God's hand was and is on this. Again, the wealth belongs to Him. I have just been assigned to *manage* it. God has given me talent as a businessman but what He has accomplished through me is not because I am a good businessman.

I used $20,000 and built a multi-million dollar health club chain. I would sound silly to myself if I said this happened because I am a good businessman. I would also be taking credit for something that obviously would not have happened if God did not do it. God accomplished this in spite of me constantly getting in the way. I tried multiple times to open the second health club by renting the building. Every attempt failed. I simply did not have the financial strength. The only way it worked was by getting an SBA loan and buying the property. We built the building from the dirt up. This turned out to be worth millions despite myself!

I actually prefer commercial real estate over residential. I like the risk reward ratio better for commercial property. That is just my preference. The upside potential for commercial real estate is much more consistent then residential real estate. Donald Trump does not buy houses, at least as far as I know. That is because it is not worth his time. That does not mean, of course, that people do not make good money buying single family homes. I just think it takes really good *instincts*. I am not confident in this area, others are. Know your strengths and apply them in your strategies.

Commercial real estate is bought and sold on capitalization rates (abbreviated "cap rates"). The higher the cap rate, the better it is for the *buyer*. The lower the cap rate, the better it is for the *seller*. This is important to recognize.

It is not hard to make good commercial real estate decisions unless the buyer or seller is uniformed. People that buy and sell commercial real estate usually have higher financial IQ's and do not make a lot of big mistakes. They know what their objectives are and they pursue them.

Many business owners who own their business and building put them up for sale *together*. These are often sweetheart deals for the buyer. In these cases the property is usually undervalued because there is no rental income. Often the business and the real estate can be purchased for much less than the actual value of the real estate alone.

Separating Businesses and their Property

I created great wealth by separating my business from the property and creating a twenty-year lease. For example, the property that housed the business appraised at $2.5 million before the separation. The mortgage payment was about $18,000 per month. The new lease I created was a *triple net lease* and started at $30,000 per month with 3% increases each year. The building was then appraised at over $5.2 million. (Remember that the value of commercial property is determined by the income it generates.) I then refinanced the property and took out $900,000 tax free, and the new monthly mortgage is about $19,000 per month. I sold the business, increased the value of the property and created significant cash flow with one move.

Leveraging Real Estate

Real estate can also be leveraged just like a business. That is why it is so popular. I will keep this example simple just like I did with the business purchase.

To understand leveraging real estate you need to understand *return on assets* (ROA) and *return on invested capital* (ROI). Leverage is what makes real estate investing seem so great. If I buy a home for $400,000 and that home goes up 5% to $420,000, I just made $20,000 on a $400,000 asset. I did not pay cash for the home, though. Let's say I put $100,000 down on the home. I made $20,000 on my $100,000 investment. That is *return on invested capital.* When the interest and tax consequences are factored in, I can figure out the true benefit which is probably even better for me.

Commercial property that generates $100,000 in yearly income selling at a 10 cap would generate a $1,000,000 purchase price. Here is the formula: divide $100,000 by .10 (100,000/.1 = 1,000,000). 40% down is a standard for commercial real estate. So the down payment is $400,000. At 7% interests amortized over 25 years the mortgage payment is about $50,890 per year. The cash generated per year is $100,000. 100,000 subtracted by 50,890 is 49,110. The positive cash flow generated the first year is $49,110. If the rent goes up 3% every year the positive cash flow the second year will be $52,890 and the third year will be $55,980. If the investment is sold after the third year at a 10 cap the selling price would be $1,060,900. In the 3 years $29,500 in principal would have been paid off. The three year profit is $248,380. That is not a bad return on $400,000 over three years.

Furthermore, there are many other variables that are to be factored in. There is a tax benefit for depreciating the building, and the proceeds could be rolled into another property. This is called a "1031 exchange." The down payment on the new property would be about $648,380. The right real estate investments can grow nicely.

I am not recommending that anyone run out and buy a business or real estate just because they have read this book. Similarly, a person sitting on the couch watching a daredevil jump ten cars on his motorcycle should not get off the couch and go try it. I have given very basic and simple examples on investing in businesses and real estate. I am not recommending one course of action but rather trying to use examples from my own financial affairs to show you ways that you could grow principle for yourself and others. Although I am not a financial advisor, I hope that my examples can demonstrate that money can be made in the right investments.

Chapter 14: Business Entities

When starting a business, a decision must be made on what type of entity to organize. In this chapter I will help the reader understand some of the entities that can be set up so that wise decisions can be pursued with greater understanding and with less fear.

One objective here is to try to receive passive or indirect income as opposed to direct income. Direct income is subject to self employment tax. Self employment tax is social security. I mentioned this earlier. Some examples of passive income are *interest income or rental income* from real estate. Direct income is from a direct payment for services provided. All income passing through to a *general* partner in a limited partnership is direct income but that same income passing through to a *limited* partner of a limited partnership is passive.

Corporate law is always changing, so remember that when setting up a business it is important to seek legal guidance. It does not cost much to set up a basic business entity but it gets more expensive as more detail is required.

The first entity I will mention is a sole proprietorship. I will not get into this one in very much detail. I will just say avoid it and leave it at that. I have been sued a lot of times. Anyone can sue you for any reason! Do not do it. Not only is a person with a sole proprietorship vulnerable, all income is direct or similar to the income received by a general partner in a partnership. People with the "poor" mentality think if someone has the guts to take a risk and is successful they are *lucky*. People with the poor mentality do not understand that taking risk is profitable. They are not willing to take risks because they are fearful. If someone else takes a risk and is successful they think they should get some of it. This makes me sick. When someone takes a risk and builds wealth, many "have-nots" think it is luck and will try to figure out a way to get lucky by taking it. Remember, many "have-nots" think money is green air and have no problem trying to take a couple breaths of what God has given others to manage.

Types of Corporations

There are two types of corporations. One is an S Corporation and the other is a C Corporation. These two entities have some similarities but in actuality are very different. One similarity is that both may have one or multiple share holders. Both have a President, Secretary, Treasurer, and board of directors. Other titles might include Chief Executive Officer (CEO), Vice President, Chief Operating Officer (COO), Chairman of the Board, etc. One person can hold all of these titles.

Income earned in an S corporation flows through to the share holders as passive income. That means the owners receive the profit directly after business expenses, and pay taxes on that profit. The income passing through to the owners is passive which means there is no self-employment tax (which would be over 15 percent).

In a C corporation, by contrast, the income earned or lost belongs to the C Corporation and all taxable income or loss is direct. This means all income is the same. Interest income is the same as consulting income and even capital gains. A C Corp never pays self-employment tax but it does pay payroll taxes. Payroll taxes are determined by the wages paid to employees and include such things as Medicare. The corporation is also required to pay half of the social security liability paid by employees.

Some states require state corporate income tax just like some states require personal state income tax. Corporations have different tax brackets just like individuals have different tax brackets.

In Limited Liability Companies, known as LLC's, income can either be passive or direct. Consulting income is an example of direct income in an LLC. Rental and interest income are examples of passive or indirect income in an LLC.

An LLC has a managing member and can have multiple owners. One reason LLC's are popular is because they offer limited liability just like the name implies. However, owners of an S Corp, C Corp, and limited partners in a limited partnership have similar if not more protection.

LLC's are popular entities for owning real estate. Most real estate owners set up an entity for each piece of real estate owned. If a court decides a building was in the way of someone with the "poor" mentality who drives their car though a building, the labor-sucking vacuum will only get one piece of property instead of *all* the properties if they are put in one entity.

Do not laugh! I have been sued over absolutely ridiculous things that I had nothing to do with. We have all heard about juries awarding hundreds of millions of dollars to a smoker that could not read the warning on a cigarette box and thought he or she was smoking vitamins. Why do you think we see silly warnings on products like, "Don't use this hair dryer while sleeping in a bath tub full of water"? Each warning either represents a lawsuit or a guess as to the next thing they will get sued over. They would not put ridiculous warnings on products if they did not think they would get sued for ludicrous reasons. This is where my wife steps in and keeps my mouth in check. When I see a commercial that starts out saying "people are smart" I know the next thing coming is the manipulation of people who are not smart. At this point my wife steps in to prevent me from proving I'm not smart either by shooting my mouth off!

The last entity I will discuss is the Limited Partnership. Limited partnerships are similar to LLC's. Limited partnerships can have multiple owners. These owners can be limited or general partners. There must be at least one general partner.

Limited partners have limited liability but very little control of the business they have ownership in. General partners have control but are very vulnerable. It is best if a general partner has nothing to lose. That is why it is wise for a general partner to be an LLC or other entity that owns nothing. A general partner of a limited partnership can be an LLC that owns one percent of the partnership.

All of the entities I have discussed can provide protection but the tax implications vary dramatically and they each affect owners very differently. When forming a business entity it is critical to seek expert legal and accounting advice. Tax laws change every year so seek advice from professionals that keep up with the changes.

Chapter 15: Business Theory

I believe everyone should develop their own business theory and ethics. Consistency builds a solid business reputation for an individual whether a person owns a business or works in one.

Putting Employees First

There are a handful of business clichés I do not like. The first one is "business is business." This is just an excuse to be unfair and unethical to others in the name of business. "It's not personal, it's business" is what I hear. That is wrong. Business is personal. It affects everyone's personal life that has a job. Business is not a war. It is about building relationships.

"The customer is always right" is another cliché that I do not care for. The customer better not always be right! Employees must come first or there will not be any customers. If businesses put the employees first the employees will treat the customer right and provide them with the best service. Businesses can not have customers without employees.

"The customer is always right" is a joke and is a sure way of going out of business if customers ever figure out a business is run with this theory. If the customer is always right everyone will be in charge and there will be no vision. Only one person can ultimately be in charge.

A number of years ago I walked into a local yogurt shop. A chipper older gentleman was working behind the counter. I ordered a yogurt and asked if I could get a topping on it. The gentleman replied, "Absolutely, the customer is always right."

"Are you serious? Are you the owner?" I asked.

"Yes I am the owner, and the customer is always right". He then gave me the yogurt and told me it would be $3.75. I thanked him and flipped a quarter up on the counter.

"Hey, it's $3.75" he said. It seems as though we had a dispute.

"I think it's only a quarter".

"Sorry it's $3.75". I said, "I think it's a quarter and you think it's $3.75. I'm the customer and you're not so I'm right. Since I'm right you must be wrong." I put another $3.50 on the counter and told the gentleman he probably should not run his business that way. As I started to walk out, I got a puzzled look from him as if to say, "This young kid is trying to teach me a lesson." Nevertheless that business was gone just a few months later.

A competitor of ours in one of our markets had their owner interviewed by a local newspaper because one of his employees punched a customer. In the interview the owner stated that he knew better than this because he had an MBA, so he knows the customer is always right. I think it is starting to be seen that "The customer is always right" is poor business theory. I understand what a business is trying to accomplish with this philosophy but the statement needs to be modified. Even if the customer is not always right, it probably is not wise to punch them.

In our health club business we built our membership base up over 15,000 people. I rarely talked to members because it was not possible to talk to them all. I let the employees do their jobs. I remember a time I did take a call from a disgruntled person. I took the call because I had heard about this person and thought it would be an amusing conversation. He said, "Your employees will not allow me in the club. I'm going to join the club but I'm not going to pay any start up fees and I'm only going to pay $19 a month because I'm the customer."

I said, "First of all you're not a customer and you're not going to be. Second, all of our customers follow the same rules as everyone else and they don't get to make them. Our staff runs the business, not you, so go somewhere else."

I am not saying you should be mean or rude to customers. My business philosophy is that employees come first. Employees need to know they are being stood up for when they execute policy correctly. The customers come second. If the employees do not come first they will not execute company policy well and there will be no customers. I want employees to enforce the rules – and at the same time to do back flips for the customers. We want to overwhelm the customer with kindness and my hope is that the employees are always right. Of course this is not always the case, but the employees must be supported first. If employees are treated with respect they will treat the customers with respect. If employees do not come first, sooner or later there will be no customers.

I worked for a large hotel chain after graduation. I worked in the spa and was taught the customer is always right. I saw employees enforcing rules for the safety of guests. I also saw guests complain to management about this. Once a complaint was registered management would offer free massages and night stays. This was *demoralizing* for employees. Many times an employee did not enforce rules because she or he knew the guest would get catered to for disputing the rules. When this happened the employee would get written up for not enforcing the rules. This created a wide separation between management and front line staff members. It was almost impossible to build a team atmosphere.

When businesses are run with "the customer is always right" philosophy it causes significant confusion, poor organization, and a weak infrastructure.

Thinking or Being Positive

I know of people who travel around attending self-help seminars and reading books on positive thinking. I am not knocking positive thinking. But there is a difference between *thinking* and *acting* positive. Acting positive requires action. If I would have just thought positive about opening a health club it never would have happened. People can think positive until they are blue in the face and all they will have is a blue face.

In 1990 I was making about $6,000 per month as a personal trainer. If I just thought positive about starting a business back then I would still be thinking about it. My income went from $6,000 a month to $2,300 a month when I made the move, but now I make $20,000 a month before I even spend a second of my labor. I do not run the business anymore so I am working on building wealth for God through other businesses and helping those in need. My labor and talents are committed to God and belong to Him.

Thinking positively is good but it is only half of what is needed:

> *"Now faith is being sure of what we hope for and certain of what we do not see"* (Hebrews 11:1).
>
> *"But someone will say, 'You have faith; I have deeds.' Show me your faith without deeds, and I will show you my faith by what I do"* (James 2:18).

Faith is being confident of having what is not yet obtained. Action is also needed or positive thinking is just thinking. People must seek God's direction and then act on that direction. That is faith. Fear prevents people from acting on their faith. If God's direction is received accurately and is acted on, huge things will happen.

Chapter 16:
Stocks and Bonds

As I move on to discussing stocks and bonds I will discuss ways that money can be made in the right kinds of investments through these avenues. This is by no means a recommendation to buy any given stock or use a particular strategy but I do hope to familiarize you with the types of investments that can be pursued.

Let's start with bonds and keep it short. I do not like to invest in bonds. Once again, I am not telling anyone not to invest in bonds. I am saying I do not. The risk is much greater than what most people realize, especially in today's environment. (I also do not think the two servants that doubled the master's money in the story Jesus told put their master's money in bonds!)

An investment in a ten year bond yielding 5% per year will go down if interest rates go up. If the bond is held and in five years the interest rates are significantly higher, the value of the bond will be significantly lower. The investment is now tied up for another five years – or a big loss must be taken. Either way the money is not working very hard in a bond. Because of this I personally do not like the risk reward ratio with bonds. I am sure there are bond traders that make a lot of money but they are not income investors.

Let me contrast bonds with stocks. Stocks increase in value *when the underlying business increases in value*. The more income a business earns, the more valuable the stock becomes. If the earnings of a business are increasing, the value of a stock will increase. A good stock picker can accurately project the future success of the business. A stock buyer believes the value of the underlying business will increase in the future. A stock seller believes the value of the underlying business will decrease in the future.

Another way to look at it is that a buyer believes the stock is being purchased for less than it is actually worth. You may have heard investors or stock traders speak about businesses or stocks being "undervalued." This is what that term is describing. If a buyer believes the chosen stock is worth $15 per share but the stock can be purchased for $10 per share it is a good investment.

Stocks are evaluated in many ways. The two general methods used are *fundamental analysis and technical analysis.* Investors and traders use these methods in many different ways and with multiple formulas. I will give an example of each.

Fundamental Analysis

With fundamental analysis the investor attempts to project earnings of a business into the future. The P/E ratio is a common tool used. This is the *price to earnings* ratio. If a stock earns 50 cents per share and each share of stock is selling for $15 then the P/E ratio is 30 (15/.5). If a stock maintains a P/E ratio of 30 for 30 years with consistent earnings, theoretically the value of the stock would double in 30 years. Similarly, if the P/E ratio of a stock is 10 it would take 10 years for the investment to double.

When we compare a stock selling at a P/E ratio of 30, which is 30 times earnings, to the investment of a private business selling at three times EBITDA, the choice seems obvious. It is obviously better to double the investment in three years as opposed to thirty years. So why would anyone buy stocks? Why have so many people made a lot of money in stocks?

If a stock is selling for $10 with a P/E ratio of 50 but doubles it's earning the next four years in a row, the stock could be selling for as much as $160 or more. There is a very good chance this stock will maintain a P/E ratio of 50 or more each year that the underlying business is doubling its earnings. If I knew a stock was going to double its earning every year, I would buy it no matter what the P/E ratio is and I would keep buying it as long as it kept doubling its earnings. No one who knows anything about stocks would buy a stock with a P/E ratio of 50 if they knew the company was not going to grow. The investment would be far better off in a savings account.

The bottom line is that stocks go up when the company consistently increases its profit. The businesses that make the most money are worth the most. A book on this subject that I highly recommend is Jim Cramer's *Real Money* (Simon and Schuster). It is an excellent book if you want to get to know stocks from a fundamental perspective. (You may have seen his show on CNBC that helps investors get a grasp on how to invest.) He is a very entertaining and funny person. I recommend reading everything you can get your hands on that has to do with investing and business. Then take action.

Technical Analysis

Investors who evaluate stocks though technical analysis look exclusively at the history of the stock price. The theory behind technical analysis is that all individual research is built into the price of the stock and it is moving in its current direction because of that. Technicians often like to buy stocks that are consistently going up. They are consistently going up because the underlying fundamentals are consistently improving. Technicians look for patterns in stock prices and try to exploit them.

No matter what systems or strategies are implemented when picking stocks there is always a chance that an individual will get their clock cleaned. For every stock purchase there is always a winner and a loser. For every stock purchase someone made the right choice and someone made the wrong choice. One person is buying, the other is selling.

One thing is almost certain: people who buy stocks without a system, strategy or reasoning will lose money. Throwing darts or buying stocks on your neighbor's recommendation will only work if someone gets lucky. In 1999 and 2000, many people were blindly investing in stocks without thoughtful reasoning and with total disregard for risk. This devastated many people's financial positions.

Doing What You Know

I will discuss some of the ways I manage the wealth and resources God has put under my management. He has given me talent and wisdom to operate in the fitness industry. He has guided me through every aspect of the industry from building a club from raw land to teaching group fitness classes. I use this ability and experience to buy, take over, operate, consult or manage health clubs. There are very few people who can do what God has given me the ability to do in this industry. Business philosophies, systems, behaviors and strategies have been developed with His guidance. God has given all believers a purpose and talents to perform the vision He has for each believer. Remember, if you are not a daredevil then do not try performing daredevil feats in your back yard just because it looks easy on television.

Fifty-percent of my financial successes are directly related to God's involvement in the project. The other 50% are related to the biblical financial principles God has taught me.

I am not recommending that people invest exactly like I do or in what I have invested in. I am just giving examples to get you thinking and motivate you to form your own strategies. What do you know? What can you learn? Have you explored opportunities to grow capital or do you tend to just make purchases that do not grow capital? I am recommending that people form strategies and act on them. Christians always have a safety net: believers have a safety net in Christ. Furthermore, failure is not fatal. Failures are learning experiences. People that do not fail do not learn.

I have capital invested with a money manager who is a good friend of mine and very good at using technical analysis. Last year this investment grew about 30%. This is similar to a hedge fund. Most of his trades are made in the futures markets. He was trained by one of the best traders in the world.

I like to buy stocks in real estate investment trust (REITs) or investment companies. REIT's are publicly held companies that own real estate. I like REIT's because I can own real estate and have it managed by real estate experts. REIT's also pay very good dividends: they can pay anywhere from a 4% to 12% dividend. As the equity in the real estate grows the dividends go up and the value of the stock goes up. The risk associated with REIT's is low. If a REIT stock goes down you can buy more and often get a higher return on the dividend. If it goes up you can take some money off the table and wait for it to go back down where you will get a higher return.

One book on REIT's that I highly recommend is *Investing in REITs* by Ralph L. Block (Bloomberg Press). This is a really solid book that will give a good understanding of how to invest in those kinds of funds. Investing in REITs is a good way for the cautious investor to get started in real estate. As with any funds, just make sure you do your research and learn about how they work before you get started.

I like investing in investment companies and financials even more than REIT's. This is because I believe the best buys are made in private businesses. Investment company stocks are called *diversified investments or close end funds.* These are a type of financial stocks. The P/E ratios are low, the dividends are high and the risk is low. These stocks usually pay dividends over 7%. Here are some symbols for anyone that wants to do further research: ACAS, AINV, ALD, and ARCC. These companies invest in other companies. They are successful because thousands of businesses come to them for money. They get to cherry-pick the best companies to invest in. The investment capital is invested in privately or publicly held businesses that have the most potential for growth and profit. The management of the investment companies usually invests in businesses they are familiar with and good at. This means their involvement will most likely improve the business they are investing in.

Investment companies invest in other businesses in the form of loans or an equity position. In many cases it is some combination of the two. This means they are getting interest on their investment plus sharing in the profit of the business.

This is similar to what I do on a personal level. I invest resources, whether time or capital, in health clubs. Others also invest in projects I am involved in. My involvement improves the business and I am rewarded. That is why I like to invest in investment companies.

Investment companies are rewarded when they cherry-pick other businesses to invest in. When they are rewarded, the stock dividends go up. When the dividends go up their stock goes up and they have more capital to invest in other business.

Let me give you a specific example. ACAS was paying a dividend of about 10 percent a year ago. The stock went up $10 and it is still paying a 7.5 percent dividend. The dividend is also increasing on a regular basis.

When market conditions cause these stocks to go down, it is a good time to buy more because the underlying businesses that are invested in are usually strong. This means when the stock goes down it is an opportunity to get a higher dividend. ACAS has gone down in a recent credit crunch in 2007, but my guess is the dividend payments will not.

Another book I would recommend is *Rule #1* by Phil Town (Three Rivers Press). He helps unpack some of the content that I am discussing here. Two factors determine the price of a stock. The first factor is the *quality of the business* and the second is the *supply and demand for the stock* of that business. If the demand for the stock of a bad business is higher than the supply, the stock will be extremely overpriced. If the demand for stock of a good and consistently profitable business is lower than the supply, the stock will be undervalued. In other words, this is a good investment opportunity.

Remember the tiddlywinks example. If everyone wants to watch me play tiddlywinks on pay-per-view, the price will be high. That does not mean I am a good tiddlywinks player – it just means everyone wants to watch me play.

Men like Warren Buffet have made billions by buying valuable businesses that fewer people want and by being very patient. The people with the highest net worth's have made money in businesses. I am not knocking real estate by any means. Robert Kiyosaki likes to make his money in real estate and he is good at it. I just think there is far more potential in businesses. A combination of the two would be even better. One key is to understand business and real estate cycles. Many people jump on the bandwagon just in time to fall off it.

When a person buys a stock, they are buying a portion of a business. The beauty of this is that stock can be bought in *any* type of business with *less risk* than starting a business. I can buy a construction company that builds single family homes, banks, mortgage companies, or any kind of real estate. If I want to own commercial real estate, I can buy a real estate investment trust (REIT) that owns commercial real estate.

Case Study: Construction

If I started a construction company in 2001, I probably made truck loads of money until 2006. If I over-leveraged my business, I would probably be broke in 2007 no matter how much money I made in previous years.

Toll Brothers (TOL) is a home builder. The stock was selling at a 52 week low of $22.65 per share in August 2007. Its 52 week high was $35.64. Its five-year high is $58.70. If I own my own construction company currently, I am probably out of business or it will take years to turn things around. This is discussed in Phil Town's book *Rule # 1*. Because I invest in stocks I can move in and out of Toll Brothers stock in about 8 seconds.

Toll Brothers has a lot of money. They probably are not going out of business – but their stock price will probably go lower. Guess what? There is a great opportunity formulating in the stock of home builders. I can own stock in a well capitalized home builder in about 8 seconds after they go through years of suffering. Sooner or later the housing market is going to explode again. When this happens I could double my money in one year. This is the same for all industries.

Money can be made in commodities the same way. Corn is a commodity. Gold is a commodity. Coffee is a commodity. Corn is not a business so it cannot go out of business. Commodities are affected by supply and demand. Sooner or later the demand for Gold is going to go down. A low for Gold is in the low $300 range. It sells for over $650 now. Wait for a commodity to crash because the supply is high and the demand is low. Sooner or later the supply to demand ratio will reverse and money will be made. Remember, commodities do not ever go out of business because they are not businesses.

Commodities are bought and sold in the futures markets. Let me emphasize that this is not easy – if it were, everyone would be doing it. Trading futures takes years of experience to be good at it. An investor must understand how the markets work or that investor could get stuck on the wrong side of a trade and get their clock cleaned.

If a believer knows God's voice and instructions and follows them perfectly, that believer will be a billionaire in short order. Of course, this is easier said than done. I am not there yet!

Chapter 17: The Value of Wisdom

Wisdom is far greater than gold, silver and money. Wealth is not even on the same scale as wisdom. Business wisdom is incredibly valuable and critical if you are investing for yourself and others.

Many people familiar with the Bible know the story of Solomon and his request for wisdom. It brought him more wealth than he could use. I believe wisdom is similar to wealth in my life. The better I steward the wisdom He has given me, the more He will give me. I do not believe God will give me more wealth to manage than I can handle. He will not give me something that will be a detriment to my spiritual health. Why would God give me a billion dollars to manage if I am not a good steward of it?

In James 1:5 God makes us a promise concerning wisdom:

"If any of you lacks wisdom, he should ask God, who gives generously to all without finding fault, and it will be given to him."

In verse six God also tells us that we need to *believe* and not doubt. In verse seven He says we should not think we will receive anything from Him if we do not believe.

This is basic. God is serving us up a home run pitch on a silver platter. Receiving wisdom is as simple as me hiding an Easter egg under the table then telling my daughter to look under the table for the egg. God is telling us to ask for wisdom. This prayer should be easy to believe. If someone cannot believe for wisdom, I do not know what to tell them.

I do not pray for anything that I am not prepared to believe or even expect. If I pray for someone's leg to grow four inches I expect the leg to grow four inches. If it does not, I am surprised. God says do not expect to receive anything if we ask and do not believe. Do not get me wrong. I have prayed for a lot of things I have not received but that did not stop me from believing. I know one thing for sure, I will not receive anything if I do not believe – because that is what God says.

I look at wisdom very similarly to wealth. God has granted me a portion of His wisdom to manage for His glory. If I am not a good steward of the wisdom He grants me He will not give me more. I crave more! I have prayed for an increase in wisdom since I was about seven years old. I pray for more wisdom with serious respect and fear of God. The latter part of that statement is important; wisdom could have been a double-edged sword for Solomon. Solomon's kingdom was eventually divided and I believe this was due in part to the arrogance that can accompany great wisdom.

As God increased my business wisdom, I felt as though I was playing soccer against a soccer team that was blindfolded. I can beat a blindfolded soccer team by myself very easily. They cannot stop me from scoring. The more wisdom God gives me, the more things people do in business seem silly, even ridiculous.

You have probably guessed the problem that wisdom can cause for me: pride. Pride is very bad. I admit I am afraid of pride. That is probably a healthy fear. I have people in my life to keep me in check on this. One of those people is my wife. I really appreciate her speaking into my life on the subject of pride. The second I start talking about how so and so "cannot count to ten" she tells me to stop. The problem is she has to tell me to stop too much! I have a lot of wisdom because I asked, but I want ten times more, and that can only happen if I become a better steward of it. A verse that has been an encouragement to me on the subject of pride and wisdom is in Proverbs chapter fifteen:

"The fear of the Lord teaches a man wisdom, and humility comes before honor" (Proverbs 15:33).

Learning Humility the Hard Way

I learned a very hard lesson when I was playing football in college. I do not want to learn that lesson again so I reflect on it often. At that time football was a big part of my life. In high school I was very small. My junior year I weighed about 115 pounds. My senior year I weighed about 125 pounds. I made all-league both years. I walked onto the field knowing I would get killed if God was not with me. My senior year we won the North Section Californian championship, and I am in the Paradise High football hall of fame.

When I played in high school it was almost like cheating! I was a defensive back. I often had a sense of what the route an opposing receiver was going to run. Every time this happened I made an interception. I constantly told anyone that would listen to me it was because of God.

By the time I was a junior in college things were different. I was a super-star. I weighed 185 pounds. I power cleaned 300 pounds, squatted 550 pounds and ran a forty yard dash in 4.6 seconds. I was the strongest player on the team (pound for pound). I had a 35 inch vertical leap. I remember thinking to myself, "I am a great football player." The next day I stepped in a hole on the field and ended my season.

I was devastated. The physical pain is probably imaginable, but I simply cannot describe the emotional pain. What was worse, I knew what I did and I could not say I was sorry enough times to the one that gave me a talent to serve Him. I abused the gift. I was selfish. I was arrogant. I was an idiot. I never want to do that again with any talent God gives me. I especially do not want to make that mistake with God's wisdom.

Chapter 18: Retirement: Avoiding IRA's & 401-K's

In this next chapter I will likely get myself in a lot of trouble with most if not all financial advisors and many if not most pastors.

I actually invest nothing in 401K plans, IRAs, or annuities. I do not invest in these things because I do not need them. As a matter of fact I think investing in these types of investments is selfish and fearful. I think God is telling at least me not to invest in these types of products. I think they are risky and I think God says they are risky:

> *"Do not store up for yourselves treasures on earth, where moth and rust destroy, and where thieves break in and steal. But store up for yourselves treasures in heaven, where moth and rust do not destroy, and where thieves do not break in and steal"* (Matt 6:19-20).

Putting money in a 401K or IRA is storing up treasures on earth for future use to take care of someone when they retire on earth. Remember Matthew 6:25-34? God does not want us to worry about tomorrow. He will take care of tomorrow: *"But if we have food and clothing, we will be content with that"* (1 Timothy 6:8). God tells us to be content with food and clothing.

I know my family and I will always have that so I do not need a 401K. I am not saying jump in front of a bus to see if God will save you. I do have health insurance. I am also not saying do not save money. I do save to help with my kids' college education, but only part of it. Saving money is a biblical principle! I am saying I am not going to tie up God's money that can't be touched until I am at least 59 and a half for a security blanket. It is too risky and could cause me to miss an opportunity God presents. God is my security blanket. Do not be a wimp by putting God's money under a rock.

I advocate saving money, not *burying* it. I save in order to *build* God's equity. God wants us to trust Him. In Exodus chapter 16 God told the Israelites to take as much manna as they needed for the day. Every person had plenty for each day but some stored more out of fear in order to insure they would have food to eat the next day. Manna that was saved for future days was filled with maggots and began to smell. If I lose millions God has given me the wisdom to help me make more tomorrow. I do not need an individual retirement account (IRA). I need God's wisdom.

Retirement is forever in heaven. This is a big reason I do not put money in IRA's or 401K's. God promises to meet all our needs on earth. The focus should be kept on building assets in heaven. We should work for God until we are dead here on earth. Most people remember the person they had a crush on in 8th grade. In 99% of the cases, that person is irrelevant and not even in the picture. Similarly, one thousand years from now it will not matter who controlled the most money on earth. What will matter is what each person did with their resources.

Chapter 19: Leadership

With an understanding of what money is and the value of labor, leadership skills will provide the next ingredient for building wealth.

Leadership is an important ingredient for harnessing and managing labor. It must be organized. Moses' father-in-law saw that Moses was trying to do all the work himself and wearing himself out. On his father-in-law's advice, Moses chose capable, trustworthy and honest men and made them leaders under him. Moses became a leader of leaders and multiplied his labor many times over:

> *"He chose capable men from all Israel and made them leaders of the people, officials over thousands, hundreds, fifties and tens"* (Exodus 18:25).
>
> If a leader sets a good example that example will trickle down and influence an organization. Being a leader is a serious responsibility:
>
> *"Obey your leaders and submit to their authority. They keep watch over you as men who must give an account. Obey them so that their work will be a joy, not a burden, for that would be of no advantage to you"* (Hebrews 13:17).

Leaders are held accountable!

The recent jury findings in the Enron case send a strong message of what is expected of leaders. The CEO and founder of Enron were found guilty even though they claimed they knew nothing about some of the activities in their corporation. Leaders have great responsibility. They are held responsible for success and failure. They must take responsibility for all actions under their authority.

Read this example of God holding leaders accountable:

> *"I lifted you up from the dust and made you leader of my people Israel, but you walked in the ways of Jeroboam and caused my people Israel to sin and to provoke me to anger by their sins"* (1 Kings 16:2).

This leader set a bad example causing followers to sin but God was angry because of the sins of the *followers*. If an employee is rude to a customer it might not be the leader's fault but it is her or his *responsibility*. The leader must address and rectify the situation. Many actions which occur in a business might be unknown by the leader and are not the leader's fault but everything is the leaders *responsibility*. Fault and responsibility are not the same. The most effective leaders take responsibility without blaming, but give credit for success to others. A leader should never say it is "not my fault," or make excuses. This will set an example of what is expected of others.

Intimidation

One definition of a leader is someone who has followers. People follow leaders for a number of reasons. Some people follow because of fear. They fear that the consequences of going against the leader could be detrimental to them. It could get them fired. The problem with leading through intimidation is that the followers will leave the organization or will become hostile toward the leader once it is safe. A loss of power on the part of the leader can make followers feel safer and begin to challenge the leader. When leading through intimidation it is just a matter of time before the leader loses effectiveness.

Vision

Some people follow leaders because they believe it is temporarily in their best interest. Followers will choose a different leader when a better opportunity presents itself with another organization. A leader will be most effective if he or she paints a vision of hope and opportunity. Followers who buy into the vision will be onboard for the long-run. Jim Collins talks about this in his book "Good to Great" (Harper Business). This is one of my favorite books. One of the major themes is getting the right people on the bus.

Once the leader paints a vision followers can get excited about, she must lay out a plan for the vision. Leading by example will demonstrate the leader's belief in the vision and be an example of what is expected of followers. Without leading by example the leader will come across as just a "boss." If the leader takes his turn cleaning the toilets the followers will follow when it is their turn.

Follow-through

A leader must always do what he says he will do. Tasks which are the leader's responsibility must be completed on time. Leaders who do not keep their commitments cannot expect followers to keep their commitments. A leader who keeps his commitments will increase production in the whole organization through leading by example. Leaders who always do what they say they will do earn respect and trust. If a leader always does what she says she will do, followers know they can take that to the bank. Followers will also feel confident and secure. Leaders who do not do what they have committed to will just be seen as hypocrites when they project expectations on followers. This will cause followers to doubt the vision and feel insecure.

Progress

Followers will lose hope and faith in the vision if progress is not tracked. Progress is tracked through setting and obtaining goals. As goals are obtained, followers will get more excited about the vision and positive energy will be spread throughout the organization. If a leader is consistently positive about the vision, that positive attitude will trickle down.

One of the most important things for a leader to remember is that leaders who perform to the level of their own expectations will earn respect and set a positive example. If a leader goes left but expects their followers to go right it is called pushing, not leading.

Chapter 20: Reaching Your Goals

"A goal without a plan is just a dream. A goal that is not obtainable is impossible. A goal that is too easy is not a goal."

(Steve Main, Total Health Club Management, page 9)

In leadership and business, realistic but challenging goals must be set. Striving for a goal is a way to measure success. The higher the goal is, the greater the accomplishment. Goals are a part of our health club business every hour of every day. We start with the goal and work backwards to see if the goal is obtainable. We work all the way down to every hour of every day.

Setting the goal is the first step. A plan must be developed to reach the goal. Once we start to build the plan, the goal sometimes becomes ridiculous. The plan exposes the feasibility of the goal. We might find that the goal is not obtainable or that it is too easy.

The next step after setting the goal is to form objectives. If the objectives are met, the goal will be obtained. Tasks must be developed in order to meet the objectives. The first is setting the goal. The second step is forming objectives. The third step is developing the tasks. Tasks are not goals or objectives because they are done by choice. Tasks are requirements. If the tasks cannot be done, the goal is impossible. If the tasks are too few or too easy, the goal is also too easy.

Once the tasks are set, all of the focus should be taken off the goal and put on the tasks. We now get to decide if we will hit our goal or not. The people who have the discipline and ability to complete all the tasks day in and day out will hit their goal. If you get lazy or lose your discipline for one day you are in jeopardy of missing the goal!

Case Study: Sales in a Health Club

The first thing our general managers do with new sales representatives is to help them set their goals. We ask how much money they want to make. We then lay out goals, objectives, and most importantly tasks. For example, let's build off a goal of $3,000 per month for a new sales rep. The rep is paid two times a month and needs to make $1,500 each paycheck. We now have one objective: make $1,500 per check. Let's say the base pay is $400 per check. The second objective, then, is to earn $1,100 in commission per check.

Let's say a sales rep gets paid 30% commission for selling a dues membership, which is a membership that pays dues monthly for a minimum of one year. In this example the rep will also get paid 10% for paid-in-full memberships. We need to set two more objectives. The rep needs to write $3,000 in new dues memberships and $2,000 in new paid-in-full memberships per pay period. 30% of $3,000 is $900 and 10% of $2,000 is $200. This will line up with the objective of the club to write seven dues memberships for every three paid-in-full memberships.

If enrollment is waived on every membership, the new rep needs to write nineteen new single-dues memberships and four new single paid-in-full memberships every pay period. The rep works six days a week, which is about 13 days per pay period. This is an average of about one and a half dues memberships a day and about 0.3 new paid in full memberships per day. We now have two more objectives: write two new dues memberships per day and a paid-in-full every third day.

The next objective is to make what we call *rotation*. That means the sales rep has the opportunity to tour a guest that walks in without an appointment. To make rotation the rep must have six confirmable appointments in the master appointment book. This is an appointment book kept by the general manager. The rep must be projecting at least 15 new memberships for the month; he or she must have at least one produced show (an appointment that was generated and showed up) from appointments the day before and have written $150 from the previous day worked.

The next step is to create *a list of tasks* that will allow the rep to meet their objectives. We have done this by creating checklists for everyone in our organization. It is a very doable list of tasks that must be done hour-by-hour. These are tasks that are tried and tested in our industry and have worked for us for many years. It is very important to understand that the checklist is not a goal or objective. It is a *requirement*. Any person who has the discipline and skill to accomplish the right tasks day in and day out will meet their objectives and accomplish their goal.

Discipline is the big key to success. Most people do not have it. All the skill in the world is useless without discipline when it comes to obtaining a challenging goal. The discipline to stay on the road map of success requires relentless focus on the tasks that must be completed in a consistent manner. Remember, any person that does not accomplish their required tasks for just one day is in danger of missing their goal.

It is possible for someone to complete the checklist completely every day and not reach the goal. If we always complete every task and reach every goal, the goal would not be a goal. It would just be a series of tasks. The tasks on the checklist might not be the right tasks for the road map to reach the goal. Many times the tasks on the checklist must be changed or modified. The person performing the tasks might not have the skill to perform the tasks at the required level. If I do everything a professional singer does in the same manner the professional did to reach the same accomplishment, it will not work. I can't sing. I do not have the ability to perform the tasks *at the needed skill level.*

I make the following statement with reasonable confidence. If I complete my checklist every day, with the right tasks performed at a high skill level, and allow enough time for the tasks to have an impact, I will obtain my goal. But when? Just as a goal without a plan is really a dream, so is a goal without a *timeframe*. Without a timeframe I will always be working toward my goal, but working toward it as if it were a dream somewhere in la la land.

We do not always obtain our goals. With discipline and focus we will always get close, at least. Anyone who applies these simple principles can make the goals in their life very real and can accomplish great things.

Conclusion

I am certainly in no position to preach. I have probably learned more by writing this book than most people who will read it. I have realized I probably break what Jesus called the greatest commandment every day: *"Love the Lord your God with all your heart and with all your soul and with all your mind"* (Matthew 22: 37). Loving God with all your mind every second of every day is tough. Jesus said the second is like the first, *"Love your neighbor as yourself"* (Matthew 22:39). Do I really love my neighbors just as much as myself every second of every day? I am hopeless without Christ's grace.

We are tempted by money every day. That does not mean we have to succumb to the temptation.

It is easy to make mistakes with money. How should I spend it? How should I invest it? Should I give money to the pan handler in front of the convenient store ... probably not, but what if I do? What financial goals should I set?"

In my current season of life I am waiting to see what doors God's vision takes me through. I have been enjoying the benefits of investing and working with other people. This is a win-win scenario. I like to be on either side of the capital equation and often a combination of the two. If I provide business expertise and others provide the capital/money/stored labor, that capital will work more efficiently and earn more for all involved, especially God.

Vision is a key component of using the resources and talents God has given us. God has a vision and purpose for our lives. If He did not, there would not be a reason for us to be here. If God's vision and purpose for our lives is *our* vision and purpose, we have taken the first step. This first step is not hard for someone that truly decides to serve God. We know if we pray for anything that is God's will, we have it. I believe it is God's will that my vision be His vision. I ask God to saturate my whole being with His vision for my life then give me a hunger and a desire for that vision. I then ask for abundant wisdom and ability to perform the vision He has for me. I also ask for a passion for that vision. I believe it is God's will that I perform His will for my life. Do you have passion for a similar vision for your life?

My hope is that you can cast aside fear and believe by following the vision God has given. Do not doubt, but rather jump on for an exciting ride with Jesus. I tell my kids, "He will never let you down. Even when you think He is letting you down, He isn't." I believe my vision and purpose is the one God has for my life as long as it does not contradict His written word. I have to believe what I pray or I might as well not pray it.

I believe that even when it seems like I am going backwards, I am not. Even if it looks like I failed, I did not. *I am now attempting to relentlessly follow God's vision and purpose for my life.* I have to let go and trust God. I have to trust that when I acknowledge Him in every decision, He will direct my path. This is exciting because even the wrong choice is the right choice when God has control. That certainly does not mean it will always be fun:

> *"Consider it pure joy, my brothers, whenever you face trials of many kinds, because you know that the testing of your faith develops perseverance. Perseverance must finish its work so that you may be mature and complete, not lacking anything"* (James 1: 2-4).

All the money I have lost is exactly what God wanted. All the money I have given to the wrong place was the right place. Trust God and do what you feel He is leading you to do and let Him worry about the rest. That is what His grace is all about. When we follow Him we are winners even if we do not get the checkers anywhere on the board.

I predict there are people past and present who are multi-billionaires but do not see it and others who have billions of dollars who are broke. Five minutes spent by one person could be more valuable than one hundred years spent by another. If you give to receive you are not really giving or receiving. Remember: motive ... motive ... motive.

While I do not expect you to agree with every method or concept I have described in this book, it is my hope and prayer that you walk away with a greater understanding of the responsibility that God has given you to manage His resources for His benefit. What an awesome opportunity and responsibility we have. Manage it well!

Recommended Reading

Pastorpreneur, by Dr. John Jackson (Baxter Press)

Leveraging Your Leadership Style: Maximize Your Influence by Discovering the Leader Within, by Dr. John Jackson and Lorraine Bosse-Smith (Abingdon)

Halftime: Changing Your Gameplan From Success to Significance, by Bob Buford (Zondervan)

In a Pit with a Lion on a Snowy Day, by Mark Batterson (Multnomah)

Rule #1, by Phil Town (Three Rivers Press)

Rich Dad, Poor Dad, (Time Warner Paperbacks)

Real Money, by Jim Cramer (Simon and Schuster)

Investing in REIT's, by Ralph L. Block (Bloomberg Press)

Good to Great, by Jim Collins (Harper Business)